I'm In Love With A Stripper…….

Stripping At It's Best

Stella Hall

Copyright © 2015 Kingdom Living Publishing

All rights reserved. No part of this publication may be reproduced or transmitted in any form or by any means without permission of Kingdom Living Publishing Company. All Scriptures have been quoted from www.biblegateway.com, KJV, NIV, and MSG versions. All others cited directly. You may visit our website at www.kingdomlivingpublishing.com.

ISBN: 978-0-9888345-2-1

DEDICATION

THIS BOOK IS DEDICATED TO EVERYONE THAT HAS EVER BEEN STRIPPED OF ANYTHING OR NEED TO BE STRIPPED OF SOME THINGS.

Part one of "I'm In Love With A Stripper... It Ain't What You Think" was published in 2011. After the publication was completed, God said to me one morning, "You did what I told you, but you did not tell the entire story. It is not about being embarrassed, it's about helping someone else." I got a little angry because I was happy that the book was finished. I really did not think that I had anything else to say on the subject matter. Well I am here to tell you that your own thoughts will get you into trouble. Here we are again, but this time, telling the complete story!

INTRODUCTION
(Similar to Book One. I had to set a foundation for the remaining of the book.)

To strip is defined by "Dictionary.com" as "to remove, make naked, undress, to deprive or dispossess; to rub, to make bare, to take apart; to damage or to break."

This book was written by me, lived out by me but inspired by God and T-Pain. In 2005, T-Pain wrote a song entitled "I'm In Love With A Stripper (Dancer)". When I first heard the song, I was lying in bed one night, in a very depressed state. I heard a small still voice tell me to cut the radio on. Me, thinking I was imagining it, turned over in bed. I thought since I could not sleep, it was just what I (my flesh) wanted to do. Playing music would sometimes soothe the pain and put me to sleep.

I heard something again say, "Cut the radio on!" This second time I said to myself, God is trying to tell me something. I had been down and depressed, maybe God is trying to pull me out of this. I had been down and depressed a little too long and just maybe God had a song to speak life into my Spirit. I was obedient, I got up, went across the room, cut the radio on and got back into my bed. I felt like I had accomplished something because obedience is better than sacrifice.

> "So Samuel said: "Has the Lord as great delight in burnt offerings, and sacrifices, As in obeying the voice of the Lord? Behold, to obey is better than sacrifice, and to heed than the fats of rams."
> (I Samuel 15:22 New King James Version)

After getting back into bed, I heard a commercial playing. Now what's going through my mind? I heard not the voice of God! I wanted to go cut the radio off, however I would have had to get out of my bed to go and cut it off. Eventually a song came on. When I heard the song, I began to get angrier because of the genre of the song. That told me that one of my kids had been in my room listening to music. One of the three of them had switched my station from Praise 100.9 to Power 98(97.9) WPEG. Because I did not want to get back up, I let the song play. The song that was playing was "I'm In Love With a Stripper" by T-Pain. I let the song play because I was comfortable and did not want to move again. I finally dozed off. I woke up around 3:45am and what was playing? You got it, "I'm In Love With a Stripper." I put the pillow over my head to try to muzzle the song because now I am getting tired of the song. When I woke up at 6:45am the song was playing again. This time I am yelling at the radio, "Can't you play anything else?"

Days passed by, but this crazy song was still ringing in my head. I caught myself even humming it a few times. One day I came home from work and my kids were in the living room watching BET. I usually go to my room so that I can regroup but I was mentally, physically and emotionally drained from dealing with problems and issues that Case Managers go through, so I just sat down on the sofa and began watching "106 and Park" with my kids. While sitting there, guess what video came on the television? "I'm In Love With A Stripper". This time I began questioning my kids about the song. They told me what the song was about and who was singing. I still thought the song was stupid.

That evening this particular Church in Charlotte, North Carolina called and asked if I would come and be their guest preacher for their youth service. In preparing for that service, I could not get a message together. I felt like God was not speaking to me. While I was studying and praying the song "I'm In Love With A Stripper" came back to mind. I began binding and rebuking the devil because I am praying and worshipping and this secular song was playing in my mind.

"Verily I say unto you, whatsoever ye shall bind on earth shall be bound in heaven; and whatsoever ye shall loose on earth shall be loosed in heaven."
(Matthew 18:18 King James Version)

Out of all the days in the world, I decided to exercise the authority God had given me and the authority that was left for me when Jesus took my very own idiosyncrasies to the cross with him. I am so grateful that He thought I was worthy enough to take my sins, errors and issues to the cross with Him. Even though He had me in mind when He went to the cross, I still have things that I must do in order to please Him. Exercising my authority is a good thing. However exercising your authority at the wrong time can get you into a lot of trouble. Being in the perfect timing of God is the most important thing. There is a time and a place for everything.

> **"To everything there is a season, and a time to every purpose under the heaven."**
> **(Ecclesiastes 3:1 King James Version)**

I heard God ask me a question very loud and clear. I thought everyone in the house heard it but no one commented. I hollered out of my room to the kids but they heard absolutely nothing. God said, "Who are you in love with?" I told God I was in love with Him. And then I heard God say, "Then what are you binding, loosing and rebuking? Did I not strip you to save you? Did I not strip you of some things to break some chains in your life?" After all of that I had tears flowing. Let me warn you, I am a very big crybaby. I began repenting for not discerning what He was trying to tell me. That experience birthed the sermon and the book "I'm In Love With a Stripper". It is a necessity that we are stripped by God. The Word of God tells us

"And those who belong to Christ Jesus have crucified the flesh with its passions and desires." (Galatians 5:24 English Standard Version).

We must die to our flesh, worldly lust and desires daily. In book one I told the world, I decided to maximize the moment and began writing my story. I kept making excuses of why I could not get it done. I missed the opportunity just like the man that laid at the pool of Bethesda that was sick for 38 years in John 5:1-14. Let's take a look at the story. Jesus went to Jerusalem. Next to the Sheep Gate in Jerusalem was a pool. The pool was called Bethesda. This pool had five colonnades. Colonnades are a row of columns supporting a roof. Under this roof lay many which were sick, blind, lame and paralyzed waiting for the water in the pool to move. (How many of you are awaiting something to happen but don't know how to make it happen or what to do when it happens). An angel was called to go down to the pool on various occasions and stir the water. The first one in the pool after the troubling of the water was healed from their illness. This man that was there had been sick for 38 years. When God saw him, he knew this man had been waiting for a long time, so he asked the man if he wanted to be healed. The man said, like many of us would have said, I don't have anyone to put me in the water and the closer I get someone gets in front of me. Jesus told the man, "get up, take up your bed, and walk."

I felt like I was the man at the Pool of Bethesda. God had spoken and told me to rewrite, but the excuse I kept saying was, I did not have money or resources right now to get the book published. One night while I kept using that same lame excuse, God said, "even if I made away for it to be published right now you would miss the moment just like the man at the Pool of Bethesda, because you have not even written the book." Boy that was a smack in my face. The reason we miss opportunities is because we have too much baggage on us and we are too afraid to let God really strip us. The stripping process is a continuous process. You are not stripped and then all of a sudden you are a perfect person. You must allow God to strip those layers away from you that are holding you captive in your mind, body and soul. Now it does not bother me that sometimes I have to go back and allow God to strip some dead skin off of me again and again and again.

"Go ahead, examine me from inside out, surprise me in the middle of the night, you'll find I'm just what I say I am. My words don't run loose."
(Psalm 17:3 The Message Bible Version)

We allow God to strip us from some things and we hold on to other things because we are afraid of being free. Dictionary.com defines afraid as "feeling fear or anxiety." Fear keeps us from many things. Fear piles on layers and layers of bondage. God strips us and takes it away from us, then we take it back and put it back on. We go to the altar for prayer and when we leave the altar we take the troubles and fear back with us instead of leaving it with God. Tye Tribbett says "the same God right now is the same God back then". If He stripped you before, He will strip you again. I'm in love with a stripper. Doing this journey of the preceding pages you will see stripping at its best.

A MIND IS A TERRIBLE THING TO WASTE

"'Very well', the Lord told Satan, 'he is in your power, only, spare his life.' So Satan left the Lord's presence and infected Job with terrible boils from the sole of his foot to the top of this head."
(Job 2:6-7 Holman Christian Standard Bible)

"There was a man in the country of Uz named Job. He was a man of perfect integrity who feared God and turned away from evil."
(Job 1:1 Holman Christian Standard Bible)

What does that Scripture have to do with wasting a mind? God said this version of "….Stripper…" is based on the book of Job. Many times we have to live out the things that we use to bring others closer to Christ. I feel personally that I have had some similar experiences of Job.

There was a statement going around and young people, teachers, principals are still quoting the statement, "A mind is a terrible thing to waste." This was a slogan used by the United Negro College Fund in 1972 during a campaign. This is a slogan still used by educators today.

Our mind is a small piece of matter but very powerful. Dictionary.com defines it best as "the element, part, substance or process that reasons, thinks, feels, wills, perceives, judges; reason, sanity or sound mental condition."

Job was a wealthy man who had

everything he could possibly want. He had seven sons and three daughters. He had 7000 sheep, 3000 camels, 500 yoke oxen, 500 female donkeys and many servants. Job had nothing to worry about, so he (we) thought. It's a verse we tend to skip over when we are studying the book of Job.

"His sons used to take turns having banquets" (today we call them parties) **"at their homes. They would send an invitation to their three sisters to eat and drink with them. Whenever a round of banqueting was over, Job would send for his children and purify them, rising early in the morning to offer burnt offerings for all of them. For Job thought: Perhaps my children have sinned, having cursed God in their hearts. This was Job's regular practice."**
(Job 1:4- 5 Holman Christian Standard Bible)

Even though Job was wealthy and had everything he could ever want, his mind was always on his children. He wanted his children to have the mind of God. He wanted their mind, body, and soul to line up with God. A mind is a terrible thing to waste. God has given you an assignment that only you can complete. If you don't complete that assignment, someone else may not live out their full potential. Imagine this, there are so many cemeteries filled with people who did not complete the assignment or purpose God created for them.

We use our mind, but not the way God intended for us to use it. Our mind controls other parts of our body. It tells other parts what to do and what not to do. Our mind is how we think and how we reason. When you are strong in your mind and you have made up in your mind to do something or not to do something, nothing can shake you or change your thinking. Many times we are not confident in our own mind. We allow people to control us through our mind. Control is defined in Webster's New World Dictionary as "to regulate or direct; to exercise authority over, to restrain or to regulate." I have said over and over no one can control my mind and I think for myself. My actions were far from that statement though. I may like a certain thing but because someone I looked up to didn't like it or say something different I would change my mind and go with them. I have allowed people to take control of me. Control can be a good thing but control can also be a bad thing. Negative control is a form of the Jezebel Spirit. Negative control will have you doing and saying things that you normally will not be doing.

When we don't operate in our own mindset and we allow others to make decisions for us and tell us step by step how we must live our lives, what we must say, where we must go, how we should act or even think, then that is a bad thing. When people control you, they are the puppeteer and you are the puppet. When we allow God to control us and not people, then we will begin to live a very fruitful life. I would rather be a puppet and God be my puppeteer anytime. You will never go wrong or astray with God leading you.

"But thou shalt remember the Lord thy God; for it is he that giveth thee power to get wealth, that he may establish his covenant which he sware unto thy fathers, as it is this day."
(Deuteronomy 8:18 King James Version)

That means we have to use our minds for God. He has equipped us in things that matter! Our assignments will be completed when we start using the mind that God has given us.

On the flip side of things, it is a necessity to lose our mind. When you lose something it is no longer a part of you. You have probably figured by now I am a definition person. Dictionary.com defines to lose as "unable to find something or someone."

Growing up as a child, I was always told a mind is a terrible thing to waste. Get all the education you can because you will need it. Because of that, I strived to make good grades. I was a very competitive person and had to do better than the person beside me. (Truth be told I am still like that today). I am not knocking education because I am a professional student and I probably will be like that till the time I leave this earth. I graduated high school, matriculated to Hampton University, quit school, later matriculated to Central Piedmont Community College, and quit school again. Finally got my Associates Degree in Biblical Studies/Theology, a certificate in Computer

Operations from PSI Institute and a BA in Psychology but because the school I went to was not accredited I am currently working on another Bachelors but this time in Criminal Justice. I did not say all of that to get a pat on the back or for someone to feel sorry for me. With our economic downfall, even those with many degrees are looking for employment just like those with no education. The unemployment rate across the world is high and high with those with degrees. Even though it has come down some, it is still high. Even though it's high, it behooves you to gain wisdom, knowledge and education.

"Listen to counsel and accept discipline, that you may be wise the rest of your days"
(Proverbs 19:20 New American Standard Bible)

Even though Job lost his mind and followed God, it didn't stop trouble from hitting his house. He prayed for his children after every party, but what Job did not know was, God had given Satan permission to attack him.

"One day when the angels came to report to God, Satan, who was the designated accuser, came along with them. God singled out satan and said, 'What have you been up to?' satan answered God, 'Going here and there, checking things out on earth.' God said to Satan 'Have you noticed my friend Job? There's no one quite like him, honest and true to his word, totally devoted to God and hating evil.' satan retorted, 'So do you think Job does all that out of the sheer goodness of his heart? Why, no one ever had it so good! You pamper him like a pet, make sure nothing bad ever happens to him or his family or his possessions, bless everything he does- he can't lose! But what do you think would happen if you reached down and took away everything that is his? He'd curse you right to your face, that's what" God replied "We'll see. Go ahead- do what you want with all that is his. Just don't hurt him.' Then satan left the presence of God."
(Job 1:6-12 Message Bible)

We must realize that satan has to get permission to try us. Satan came to God and asked could he attack and God said sure, they won't turn their back on me! Satan felt that Job was only being faithful to God because he had everything and surely if he attacked him, Job would turn his back on God. That is so true in so many instances. I had to take a look back at that. Many times we get so unfocused when things are going like we would have for it to go. Money is in the bank, kids acting right, spouse is happy, job is great and we tend to forget about having communion with God. But as soon as trouble hit, we are on our knees crying and begging God to intervene in the midst of our situation. Stop pimping God and using Him for your own personal magician when you need Him. I can speak on that because I was guilty of that as well.

After satan got permission from God to attack Job, his children were having another party and Job began getting news after news. First his oxen were plowing and his donkeys were grazing and the Sabeans came and attacked. Then secondly bolts of lightning struck the sheep and the shepherds and killed them. Thirdly the Chaldeans came and raided the camels and killed the camel drivers. And fourthly a tornado came and struck the house where all his children were partying and killed all the children. With all of the news Job mourned, ripped his clothes, shaved his head and fell to the ground and worshipped God, by saying

"Naked I came from my mother's womb, naked I'll return to the womb of the earth. God gives, God takes. God's name be ever blessed."
(Job 1:21 Message Bible)

Not one time did Job sin, complain, curse, cuss or anything. He kept a clear head and continued to worship and love God. If all of that had happened to us, many of us would have thrown in the towel and given up. When things like this happen to us, we begin to murmur and complain instead of praising and worshipping Him because we know that God has already worked it out. Many things are not our fault that we go through. It is because God has given the enemy permission to attack us. Sometimes losing our mind is a good thing as long as we take on the mind of Christ.

"For who hath known the mind of the Lord, that he may instruct him? But we have the mind of Christ."
(I Corinthians 2:16 King James Version)

Are we really operating with the mind of Christ? Job showed us he had the mind of Christ because he worshipped during his trials, he worshipped during his tribulations and he worshipped while things were good in his life. Worship is an important part of our relationship with Christ. When you have the mind of Christ you will continue to look towards the hills because that is where your help comes from, the Lord.

"I will lift up mine eyes unto the hills, from whence cometh my help."
(Psalm 121:1 King James Version)

Someone is probably saying, how could

Job have the mind of Christ when he was born before Christ? We must remember that God the Father, Jesus (Christ) the son, and the Holy Spirit were all here from the beginning of time.

"Then God said, "Let us make man in Our image, according to Our likeness; and let them rule over the fish of the sea and over the birds of the sky and over the cattle and over all the earth, and over every creeping thing that creeps on the earth."
(Genesis 1:26 New American Standard Bible).

Job had to really have the mind of Christ because after all that trouble he had, more came his way.

"One day when the angels came to report to God, satan also showed up. God singled out satan, saying, 'And what have you been up to?' Satan answered God, ' Oh, going here and there, checking things out.' Then God said to satan, 'Have you noticed my friend Job? There's no one quite like him, is there- honest and true to his Word, totally devoted to God and hating evil. He still

has a firm grip on his integrity! You tried to trick me into destroying him, but it didn't work.' Satan answered, 'A human would do anything to save his life. But what do you think would happen if you reached down and took away his health? He'd curse you to your face, that's what.' God said, 'Alright go ahead. You can do what you like with him. But mind you, don't kill him.' Satan left God and struck Job with terrible sores. Job had ulcers and scabs from head to foot. They itched and oozed so badly that he took a piece of broken pottery to scrape himself, then went and sat on a trash heap, among the ashes. His wife said, 'still holding on to your precious integrity, are you? Curse God and be done with it!' He told her, 'You're talking like an empty headed fool. We take the good days from God, why not also the bad days?"
(Job 2:1-10 Message Bible)

Not once through all this did Job sin. He said nothing against God. When you have not allowed God to strip your mind and replace the emptiness with the mind of God then you would be like a ship tossing with no sail.

Be honest with yourself. Would you be

like Job or would you have given up by now? Just like Job's wife, we have spouses, boyfriends, girlfriends, lovers, etc. speaking that same negativity into our own lives and we allow that to disturb our integrity. When I was married and knew that God was calling me to the ministry, I told my ex-husband my experiences and he stated he did not want to be married to anyone in ministry, so I delayed the vision God had given me till years after that. When you have the mind of Christ you should be like Isaiah and say

"Remember ye not the former things, neither consider the things of old. Behold I will do a new thing now it shall spring forth; shall ye not know it? I will even make a way to the wilderness and rivers in the desert."
(Isaiah 43: 18-19 King James Version)

Once we get stripped from the inside out then we can faithfully chase after God. You should have a yearning to want the mind of Christ. Our minds are so cluttered with so much junk that we can't be stripped by God.

I shared this story in my first book and feel the need to share it again. I grew up between houses. It made me a bitter unhappy individual. I loved living with my aunts and grandparents, but that did not compare to me wanting to be with my mother and father. I felt unloved and unwanted. My relatives were great to me. I did not want for anything but that was nothing like being in a home with my parents. I use to wonder why they took my baby sister with them and left me. Many times I wanted to run away because I did not feel loved. That stayed with me straight into my grown up years and I began to have major self-esteem issues. I ran away from many things in life because of low self-esteem. Self-esteem is a beast and is killing many people because they do not know how to handle it. When we don't deal with the root of a problem it follows us to every journey we take in life. Because my self-esteem was low, I pretended I was on the up and up. I wore a mask and it was not even Halloween. A mask is defined in Webster's New World Dictionary as "a covering to conceal or protect the face; anything that conceals or disguises." Many of us, (you reading this and I) wear masks daily. We want to hide who we really are because we don't like the person we see when we look in the mirror. All of my low self-esteem issues made me feel unloved. After all they took my sister and moved to Georgia and left me in Charlotte NC. What I did not care to know or understand was my father's job transferred him to Atlanta, Ga., and because I was in school, they left me in NC and went on to Ga. This reminds me of a passage of Scripture in the Bible.

"Don't let this bother you. You trust God. Don't you trust me? There's plenty of room for you in my Father's home. If that were not so would I have told you that? I'm on my way to get a room ready for you."
(John 14:1-3 Message Bible)

My father had gone to Georgia to prepare a place to bring me to and I did not understand that.

A mind is a good thing to waste. When you are stripped of your mind you will no longer think on your own. You can no longer make decisions on your own. When you put on the mind of Christ, you allow Him to lead, guide, direct, make decisions and order your mind. The Word of God tells us to pray continuously.

When Job heard all of the bad news that was coming to him back to back, he ripped his clothes, shaved his head, fell to the ground and worshipped and prayed. And said,

"Naked I came from my mother's womb, naked I'll return to the womb of the earth God gives, God takes. God's name be forever blessed."
(Job 1:21 Message Bible)

When satan saw that after Job had lost everything and still didn't give up on God, he felt some type of way. When you have on the mind of Christ, nothing, no obstacle, no trial, no tribulation will take your mind off of Christ. You will continue to pray. You will continue to serve. You will continue to praise. You will continue to worship because you know who's you are and who is keeping you. When you have on the mind of Christ it does not matter what wind blows in, you are still

"...steadfast, unmovable and always abounding in the work of the Lord, for as much as ye know that your labour is not in vain in the Lord."
(I Corin 15:58 King James Version)

People may not understand you because you have been stripped of your own mind and you have taken on the mind of Christ. Don't worry about that. People will talk about you, they talked about Jesus. They can talk about you and do all matters of evil against you but because you are standing firm with the mind of Christ, nothing will be able to hold you back. He is preparing a table for you in the presence of your enemies.

> "Thou prepares a table before me in the presence of mine enemies; thou anointest my head with oil; my cup runneth over."
> (Psalm 23:5 King James Version)

Nothing will be able to shake your faith. The enemy may try and he will get into the people that is the closest to you and they don't even know they are being used by satan. When you try to tell them, you will be the one at fault, so do you and be God with your stripped mind. Remember what Isaiah said.

> "No weapon formed against you shall prosper, and every tongue which rises against you in judgment, you shall condemn."
> (Isaiah 54:17a New King James Version)

In Chapter 2 of Job, God had another meeting with the angels and satan showed up again. God asked him again what have you been up to and satan told him again, going here and there, checking things out. God again offered to satan Job, because he had confidence that Job would not falter. He would not be wishy washy. My question to you is does God have confidence in you? Can God offer you to Satan and be confident that you will hold fast and not waiver? Satan told God a person would do what he needed to do to save his life. God still believed that Job would be faithful and gave satan permission to touch his body but he could not kill him. As I previously stated God will use the one closest to you to cause you to waiver.

When we are going through things our attitude has a lot to do with our messed up minds. Our attitude will dictate how we will treat, love or hate others. Our attitude can lead or mislead us just like our mind can lead or mislead us. When you are operating in your own mind, you will always think opposite of how things really are. When this occurs, the mind has not been transformed.

I must confess my mind has been all messed up. I thank God for delivering me. I was a total wreck. Low self-esteem, depression and unhappiness had my mind all tied up, tangled up and wrapped up in mess. Early in the chapter I spoke of always wearing a mask. I pretended to be happy even when I did not feel like it. I was taught that you don't show people or tell people what's going on with you. My maternal grandmother use to say, "Don't air your dirty laundry for others to see." I was trapped inside of my own body. So many times I tried to break free. I did not know how nor did I know who to ask for help. All through my elementary school days I strived to get good grades so someone would be proud of me. I learned to read before I could talk plain. My maternal grandfather was a Pastor and before I started kindergarten I was reading the Bible to him. I was in the

Charlotte Observer Newspaper in Kindergarten because I was well advanced and the teacher had a hard time finding things for me to do. I was in the Charlotte Observer Newspaper again when I was in second grade for reading the most books out of all the students in The Charlotte Mecklenburg School System. At the end of my second grade year I was promoted from second grade to fourth grade because I had already completed all of the third grade work. I was still unhappy because my parents were not with me but it wasn't as bad as I thought. The summer after my second grade year I was elated because my father came from Georgia to get me and took me back with him. Well after the first few nights I was back to my depression, my sister was with me, my daddy was with me but my mom was not with me. I was missing a familiar sound that I went to sleep to at night when I went to sleep. That was the sound to my parents talking or arguing. I did not know where my mom was and when I asked no one knew. Here I was, I had prayed to God every night to send me to Atlanta to my family and He did, but my mom was not with me. Things were not the same. My dad loves his girls, so he treated us very good. Because I pictured happiness to be my mom, my dad and my sister and I and that is not how it was, I thought my family was abnormal. I cried at night so no one could see or hear me, all I wanted was happiness. Depression hit me again. My mind was so unsettled even as a third grader. I had a habit of taking on things that did not belong to me. I had a habit of trying to be everything to everybody even at a young age of eight years old. When I said my mind was unstable, it didn't just begin as an adult it started with me as a little girl.

Not only was I dealing with my mom being gone, I was beginning to feel dumb. Remember I told you all of the accomplishments I had accomplished and I was only eight or nine years old. This now begins the beginning of what I thought was my fourth grade year to only find out they put me back in third grade because Georgia didn't believe in skipping grades during that era. I felt like I was dumb and failed. Depression must be dealt with and not just passed over, covered up or ignored. We, especially African Americans, don't deal with mental health issues to well. A mind is something special. Our mind will lead and guide us and when we are unstable. Our mind will get us into trouble. When you are so depressed, your mind will send you places you do not want to go like, fornication, adultery, drugs, alcohol, abuse and/or suicide. I chose suicide. I was tired of the ups and downs. I was tired of being unhappy. Things were going all wrong for me. Many things were because of my own choices but I could not see that at the time. So I took my ex-husbands gun off the top shelf of my bedroom closet and proceeded to take my own life. While I was crying and about to pull the trigger, a small still voice spoke to me and told me to look up. When I looked up all I saw was my son who was six and my daughters who were three and one asleep on my bed. The voice then said if you do this, who will take care of them like you will? Who's going to be there to assist them with their issues they will go through in life? In my head I also heard a voice say, they will be taken care of better than you are doing now. They don't need a manic depressed person as a mother. Do it! While the other voice said don't do it! There was a war going on in my head. I couldn't take it, I dropped the gun, ran to the phone and called my Pastors and told them what was going on. They immediately told me to meet them at the Church. Since I am still here to tell this story you see which voice won the battle. The voice of the Lord. And the Lord shall always win if you yield to the Holy Spirit. I was blessed. Many other situations similar to mine did not turn out that way, so I am very grateful.

I thank God for the ability to listen to the Spirit. Satan had a meeting with God and He gave satan permission to attack me. Just like Job, during my trials and low periods of life, friends walked out on me, talked about me and tried to control my life.

I thank God for transforming my mind after the mind of Christ. Transformation is defined in Webster's New World Dictionary as "to change the condition, character, or function of." Minds need to be completely transformed. Sometimes we can be so educated and we feel like we got it all together and can't nobody tell us anything but we have to lose our mind and be stripped of our thinking. Transformation is the very key in losing your mind.

"I beseech you therefore, brethren by the mercies of God, that ye present your bodies a living sacrifice, holy, acceptable unto God, which is your reasonable service. And be not conformed to this world but be ye

transformed by the renewing of your mind, that ye may prove what is that good and acceptable and perfect, will of God. For I say, though the grace given unto me, to every man that is among you, not to think of himself more highly than he ought to think; but to think soberly, according as God hath dealt to every man the measure of faith."
(Romans 12:1-3 King James Version)

We need to allow God to do a work on our minds. There are so many people in the Body of Christ still messed up in their minds. Looking good on the outside, pretending to be more than they are but broken on the inside.

Attachments are serious. When you are attached to things you are stuck to it. Attachment is defined as "an extra part or extension that is or can be attached to something to perform a particular function" by dictionary.com. Many times we are attached to people that can really help us but because of our very own mindset we can't get the help we need. The Word of God tells us that the strong are to bear the infirmities of the weak.

"We who are strong must be considerate of those who are sensitive about things like this. We must not just please ourselves."
(Romans 15:1 New Living Translation)

Seek God and don't be afraid to receive help from those that are genuinely trying to help you. Don't be so quick to say, "they just want in my business". Some people are genuinely trying to assist you. If you are operating with the Holy Spirit on the inside, your discernment should kick in on who is good for you and who is not.

Experiences can cause our mind to go haywire, especially when our success seasons are very short while our seasons of trials, tribulations, lack, hurt and pain are very long. Our mind begins to tell us "All good things must come to an end. If it ain't one thing it's another. I am destined for doom." We must realize we can define our lives by every thought and word we do or say. Change can only come when we allow God to strip every unpleasing thought and every doom and gloom thought that comes to mind. We need to be stripped!

I know that I am not the only person that have asked God to remove some things from me and when He does, we miss it so much that we take it back. I was playing "Double Dutch" with God. We all have done it. Not just one time. Not just twice but over and over and over again. When I was battling self-esteem, my mind was unstable. If someone told me the grass was purple and I knew without a shadow of a doubt that the grass was green, I would tell people the grass was purple. Mind games are a very serious thing. We allow mind games to prevent us from having or living a very fruitful life. The Word of God has the power to realign anything that is out of line including our messed up, faulty mindsets. Quit talking about living successfully and be success.

Stop thinking about having money and live a prosperous and wealthy life.

> "Remember that God, your God, gave you the strength to produce all this wealth so as to confirm the covenant that he promised to your ancestors—as it is today."
> (Deuteronomy 8:18 Message Bible)

You are what you think. Your mind does two things, build you up or tear you down. Fill your mind with the Word of God. You can't go wrong with that! You will be built up every time.

> "For I know the thoughts that I think toward you, says the Lord, thoughts of peace and not evil, to give you a future and a hope."
> (Jeremiah 29:11 King James Version)

Bobby Brown has a song called "Poison". Our very own minds are poisoning us and stunts our growth. Allow God to strip the poison from your mind, because poison can kill you. When you intake poison, you must immediately call 9-1-1. When you intake poison spiritually you must call 9-1-1. That 9-1-1 is J-E-S-U-S!

Everything in the natural begins with a thought. Before anything could be invented, the inventor had to think about his/her project before they could put it on paper. What occupies your mind determines what come out of your mouth. Allow your mind to shift. Shift your mind from negativity to positivity. God has designed our minds to create, innovate and strategize.

"I will put my instructions deep within them, and I will write them in your hearts."
(Jeremiah 31:33 New Living Translations)

The Law of Attraction says like attracts like. Once you engage in negativity, more negativity comes. Once you recognize that God has stripped your mind you can then say

"You must fix your thoughts on what is true, and

honorable and right and pure and lovely and admirable. Think about things that are excellent and worthy of praise."
(Philippians 4:8 New Living Translation)

How do I transform my mind? God is the only one that will be able to do that. You must have a close walk with him. You must also have a made up mind that you want to take on the mind of Christ and be stripped of your own mind. You must renew your mind and soul to the Lord.

Every day we are required to re-commit, re-surrender, re-submit and re-align our minds to God. If you change your attitude God will change your mind. When He strips you of your mindset you will be obedient to the Word of God. When He strips you of your mindset you will love in spite of, unconditionally. When He strips you of your own mindset, you will watch what you are thinking. One day my family got together and all of the kids were outside playing. My cousin's baby girl ran into the house crying.

She said my little nephew punched her. My brother called my nephew in and asked why did he punch her? My nephew who was five years old said, "because she was thinking about my business." We should be like that and be cautious of what we are even thinking.

"Casting down imaginations and every high thing that exalteth itself against the knowledge of God, bringing into captivity every thought to the obedience of Christ." (2 Corinthians 10:5 King James Version)

Pulling down or casting down thoughts that come to your mind that are not like Christ is how you watch what you think. Stop and take a moment and spend time with God and let him strip you of your mind. Allow God in to strip your mind, with no distractions or concerns. There is a stripping of the mind going on, are you in line for it? What you think can change your life forever.

What's Love Got To Do With It?

"Why does God bother giving light to the miserable, why bother keeping bitter people alive, Those who wait in the worst way to die, and can't, who can't imagine anything better than death, who count the day of their death and burial the happiest day of their life? What's the point of life when it doesn't make sense, when God blocks all the roads to meaning?
(Job 3:20-23 Message Bible)

Three of Jobs friends came to see him after hearing about his fate. They didn't expect to see what they saw. They could hardly recognize their good friend. They moaned with him. They ripped their robe, they cried, and they also put dirt on their heads as signs of grief. They sat with him on the ground for seven days and nights without mumbling one word. In my opinion that was love for a friend. Job finally broke the silence by cursing the day he was born and the night he was conceived but He loved God so much that he never cursed God, even though it was suggested by his wife.

Have you ever gone through so much that you wished you were dead? Have you wondered why so many bad or evil people continue, as we think, keep getting blessed? Many of us have. God loves everyone in spite of the things that we do. What does love have to do with this? Love has a lot to do with everything. God loved us so much that He gave His only begotten Son for every one of us.

Love is an emotion that involves our heart. In order to become a true vessel of God you must allow Him to strip you from your heart. Heart is defined by Webster's New World Dictionary as "the central, vital, or main part; core; the center of emotions, personality attributes." I have heard people say "I cannot cut my heart on and off and it is a must I guard my heart with my total being." Because of the lack of love, I thought I had from my parents brought on the Spirit of Abandonment. And because of that I searched for love in all of the wrong places.

> **"So don't get ahead of the Master and jump to conclusions with your judgments before all the evidence is in. When he comes, he will bring out in the open and place in evidence all kinds of things we never even dreamed of inner motives and purposes and prayers. Only then will anyone of us get to hear the 'well done of God'"**
> **(I Corinthians 4:5 Message Bible)**

Our hearts host our inner motives. We may not be able to control what enters or exits from our heart, but we sure can handle how we deal with it.

I am sure Job loved his wife but she suggested to him that He curse the same God that blessed him tremendously. He had to find a way in his heart to deal with her because of her statement.

I can imagine Job's heart was elated that his friends came from their various countries just to be with him. It probably made him even more elated that they came and sat with him and did not say a word. But his heart probably did a somersault when Eliphaz spoke up. He reminded Job of all the times he has encouraged those that were about to quit. He reminded him of how he has helped so many people and gave them hope. He spoke of how the life he has lived should give him hope during his hard times. After all that encouraging in a nutshell, he was talking against God in Job 4-5 to Job. At this stage I imagine some dislike of Eliphaz building up on the inside of Job because of this. Eliphaz told Job go to God and apologize for whatever he has done, so God can forgive him and stop all of this turmoil. Job listened attentively. When He had the opportunity to finally speak, he told Eliphaz, he did nothing wrong. Even though all of this has happened, he will leave this earth with the dignity that he did not curse God. He told his friends that they came out of love but they were fickle. They came, but when they got there, they got scared. Job also told them he had not asked them for anything but if they can find where he went wrong please tell him. Bildad, Job's other friend, out of love, said the same thing. He told him to apologize. He reminded him that his kids had sinned and they were dealt with because of their sin. Job again went off on Bildad. Job's friend Zophar went in on Job. He told Job he has not gotten half of what he deserves. If he washes his hand to sin, God will show mercy. Like the others Job went in. He told Zophar with his educated self, he must speak from the wisdom from all the educated ones but he has education too and he talks with God for himself. So many times we find ourselves in a position like this. A few years back (and we will discuss this later in latta chapters) my oldest daughter was in the hospital sick. I was at the hospital because she had just had a biopsy completed. I received a phone call that my other daughter got hurt in her basketball game and they were on the way to bring her to the Emergency Room, at the hospital I was currently in. I had one upstairs and one downstairs and we found out that she had a bad sprain. One of my friends called to check on the oldest daughter and I began telling her about the baby girl. She listened, then she said, "Stella, have you checked your life to see what is going on?" I thought first, "What the what?" I told her just because this is happening, does not mean there is something wrong with me. But that seed that was sown, really stayed with me because I started having all kinds of thoughts enter into my mind. What have I done to cause so much to happen to my kids?

Your heart causes the many emotions that we experience such as happiness, sadness, love, hate, etc. Many people enter relationships with their heart, instead of learning the other person first. Angela Bassett and Laurence Fishbourne played in a movie called, "What's Love Got To Do With It." They were re-enacting the life of Tina Turner (Anna Mae Bullock) and Ike Turner. Tina loved Ike so much that she settled just to keep her lifestyle she created. She was one of the best singers in her time. She was very anointed from a child but that did not stop the trouble from coming. Even though Ike beat her, she stayed with him. Even though Ike mistreated her, she still stayed in the relationship. It was not until Tina came in contact with her inner self and emotions that she asked herself, "What does love have to do with this?" Eventually she fought back and left Ike and all of his abuse. The only thing she wanted out of the relationship was her name. She built that name while being with Ike. When you get sick and tired of a situation you will do something about it. Change cannot occur till you are good and tired of the way it is. Things don't change till you get sick and tired of being sick and tired.

There are so many relationships we have gotten into and we have allowed our heart to lead the relationships. We can shut our hearts off and on at the drop of a dime.

"Keep thy heart with all diligence for out of it are the issues of life."
(Proverbs 4:23 King James Version)

We have to guard our hearts because that is where life start. Without our heart functioning there is no life. I know this is not a relationship book, then again it is because it deals with our relationship with God, but I feel the need to testify of the relationships (love, friend, work, church, etc.) I have been in that has caused damage to my heart because I allowed it. We are so quick to always blame a failed relationship (love, friend, work, church) on the other party. We have a lot to do with the failing of that relationship as well. I was not comfortable with myself so I let people, male or female treat me how they wanted to treat me. Because I had lack of love for myself, it did not matter what people said or did to me, I continued to stay attached and go back for more abuse. Take a good look at yourself. When you are honest and open with yourself, that is when God can really do a change with you and through you. Obedience to God is better than sacrifice of time, treasure, and talent to anyone else.

Just like the mind, the heart is an important organ needed in our body. There are many people today that have had heart transplants. A heart transplant is needed when a heart, that is not functioning as it should, is replaced with a healthy heart from a donor that died. When the heart no longer works as efficiently as it should and a person's life is at risk, a transplant is needed. The heart failure may have been caused by a coronary heart disease, hereditary, viral infections in original heart, and damaged heart valves and damaged muscles. "Every year in the United States there are about 4000 people who can benefit from a heart transplant. However there are only 2000 of those 4000 donors available." Not only are people getting heart transplants but they are having double and triple bypass open heart surgeries. Bypasses are done to treat heart attacks and chest pains. They are also getting stunts and pace makers put in to assist the heart in functioning the correct way. (www.medicinenet.com/heart_transplant/page2.htm) Why is all of this needed? It is needed because there is a malfunctioning of the heart in the lives of the people.

Malfunction is defined in dictionary.com as "to function imperfectly or irregularly or fail to function." The heart is about 5 inches long and weighs 9-11 oz and is about the size of your fist. This little muscle pumps approximately 17,000 qts of blood a day. Every cell in the human body need oxygen to live by and to function. The function of our heart is to deliver the oxygen to every cell in the body. The heart is a pump. Transplants are needed when the heart can no longer pump well enough to supply blood with oxygen and nutrients to the organs of the body. Some people have good pumps but a bad electrical conduction system of the heart. This system determines the rate, the rhythm, and the sequence of the heart muscle. The number one killer of people is Heart Disease. (www.cdc.gov)

So many of us try to do right to make sure we have a healthy heart and not have a physical heart attack. So many people, including you reading this and myself are walking around with great health. We have no issues and still have a malfunctioning of the heart. We are about to have a Spiritual Heart Attack. All of the things or issues that are in your heart you don't want to deal with. The many things we have in our heart is harboring and infesting our heart. Your daddy and mother separating or divorced, bitterness or hatred you have for someone, your spouse leaving you, physical abuse, sexual abuse, domestic violence, control, attitudes, molestation, death, etc. are all building up in your heart causing heart failure. We have so much embedded down in our heart because we have never dealt with it. God has purpose for each and every one of us and we can't even be used effectively by God unless we allow Him to strip us of our heart and give us a heart after his. God wants to strip us all of our old heart and give us a heart transplant. Without the transplant we will not be able to love God. Without the transplant we will not be able to live. We will be Spiritually dead. Spiritual death can end up in physical death.

"And the Lord thy God will circumcise thine heart, and the heart of thy seed, to love the Lord thy God with all thine heart, and with all thy soul, that thou mayest live." (Deuteronomy 30:6 King James Version)

Without the transplant you will not be able to love people.

"Ye have heard that it hath been said, thou shalt love thy neighbor, and hate thine enemy. But I say unto you; Love your enemies, bless them that curse you, do good to them that hate you, and pray for them which despitefully use you, and persecute you; that ye may be the children of your Father which is in heaven; for he maketh his sun to rise on the evil and on the good, and sendeth rain on the just and on the unjust. For if ye love them which love you, what reward have ye? Do not even the publicans the same? And if ye salute your brother only, what do ye more than others? Do not even the publicans so? Be ye therefore perfect; even as your Father which is in heaven is perfect." (Matthew 5:43-48 King James Version)

A heart transplant is essential in order to be stripped from our previous heart. In the 36th chapter of Ezekiel the Lord spoke through the Prophet Ezekiel to the nation of Israel about bringing them from their rebellious state so God can bring the glory back to himself. In order for that to happen God told them He will give them a new heart.

"A new heart also will I give you, and a new spirit will I put within you: and I will take away the stony heart out of your flesh, and I will give you an heart of flesh." (Ezekiel 36:26 King James Version)

David was a man after God's own heart but he failed in his walk. Because of the lust in his heart he broke at least 4 of the Ten Commandments. 1) Thou shalt not kill 2) Thou shalt not commit adultery 3) Thou shall not covet 4) Thou shalt not bear false witness. Even though he broke the commandments, the Word of God still say David was a man after God's own heart.

"And when he had removed him, he raised up unto them David to be their King; to whom also he gave their testimony, and said, I have found David the son of Jesse, a man after mine own heart, which shall fulfil all my will."
(Acts 13:22 King James Version)

What does it mean to be a man or woman after God's own heart? It means your life is in unity with God. What is important to Him becomes important to you. You will do everything that He ask you to do. You take the blame and responsibility of your own actions and not throw it off on someone else. When God tell you to go to the left, the right or stay straight you are obedient and will do just that. When God tell you to stop doing a certain thing, you immediately do it with no hesitation. When you are a man or woman after God's heart, you are sensitive to the Spirit of God. When you are a person after God's own heart, you understand that you are a Worshipper!

> **"God is always on the alert, constantly on the lookout for people who are totally committed to him. You were foolish to go for human help when you could have had God's help."**
> **(II Chronicles 16:9 Message Bible)**

David went after another man's wife. David lied and deceived his best military man to cover up his affair with the man's wife because she was pregnant with his child. David had the man killed to justify his own wrong doing. He was all of that and God was still able to use him mightily throughout the Word of God. David taught us humility and how to Worship God in Spirit and in Truth. Why was it so easy for God to use this man that society would classify in today's time as a very bad person? David was able to admit that he needed a heart transplant and he need God to be the Chief Surgeon. He was able to admit he needed to be stripped of his own heart. He asked God to wash him whiter than snow and create in him a clean heart.

> **"Why art thou cast down, O my soul? and why art thou disquieted in me? Hope thou in God: for I shall yet praise him for the help of his countenance."**
> **(Psalm 42:5 King James Version)**

Do we actually trust that? No! We have guilty feelings because we don't fully trust that God is in control. It is so easy to hide your heart by dressing up, by flaunting the finer things in life and by your success but deep down inside you have a heart that is hurt and bleeding. Many people are disappointed, relationships failing, lonely hearts, sick in body, sick of life, etc. God sees what's in your heart and he loves us and wants to heal our broken hearts.

> **"But when he saw the multitudes, he was moved with compassion on them, because they fainted, and were scattered abroad, as sheep having no shepherd."**
> **(Matthew 9:36 King James Version)**

God wants to love us and He wants us to love everyone. Love is the greatest commandment. When you create something, you are redesigning or starting from scratch. Webster Dictionary defines create as "to cause to come into existence; to make originals." Every time you say 'Create in me a clean heart', God makes you a new heart. We must allow God to strip us from our heart so it can be pure and holy before Him.

The question, "What's love got to do with it" is a valid question.

**"They are inclosed in their own fat: With their mouth they speak proudly."
(Psalm 17:10 King James Version)**

You may not want to believe me and think that I am just writing something, but I have been there. I pretended and wore a mask for so long that I just gave lip service and closed my heart right up. If I be honest there are times now when people have really gotten the best of me, I can still shut my heart off. I have to pray often that I don't stop loving in spite of how people treat me. It is a daily process.

In the natural heart failure can be caused by Diabetes. Diabetes occur because either you have to much sugar in your blood stream or not enough sugar in your blood stream. That happens because you do not have a proper diet. In the spiritual heart failure can be caused by Spiritual Diabetes. Spiritual Diabetes occur because of an imbalanced diet of God's truth. Are you studying the Word for yourself? Are you actively listening to the Word of God and not just hearing the Word?

Many people believe that because they have a stony heart, or a not so perfect heart, they cannot be used by God. Don't think like that! As long as you can admit what is going on with you, God can rebuild you. How many people in the Bible did God use and they had flaws, issues or problems? All of them! He can mold you. He can give you a heart of love. Love has a lot to do with everything. Love went to the cross for us. Love heals. Love can pick you up and it can deliver. Love will cleanse you. "When nothing else could help, love lifted me."

It is time that we deal with the issues of life that we have harbored so long. We are looking for love in all of the wrong places and our heart have nothing to do with what we do or places we go, when we are operating out of the will of God. When we have been abused, molested, or even mistreated, we go after things to try to cover up what we have been through instead of dealing with it. I didn't harbor hatred but I should have because I was harboring so much on the inside of me, that it was stopping me from growing in God, even as a Minister. Stop being mad at people. You are mad at some people and God has called them on to glory and you still hating them. Let it go! Allow God to empty out of you all of those things that are keeping you from moving forward. When you unpack a suitcase, the suitcase becomes light. Allow God to unpack the suitcase of your heart and take out all the baggage that has become a weight in your heart. God can strip you and He is the only one that can strip you, create in you a clean heart, and renew a right mind in you so that you can live an effective, fruitful and abundant life for Him.

Many times we cannot love because our hearts have not healed from being broken or hurt. We spoke of earlier in this chapter the many ways our heart can be fixed. If a person has to go through a situation like a bypass, transplant, etc., the doctor will tell you the importance of keeping your heart fit, the importance of changing your diet and the importance of exercising. We have heard the statement, "so it is in the natural, so it is in the spirit."

"Then I will sprinkle clean water upon you, and ye shall be clean: from all your filthiness, and from all your idols, will I cleanse you."
(Ezekiel 36:25 King James Version)

You must be cleaned up. David did not have

a problem in telling God to create in him a clean heart. Exercise your authority and come to God in sincerity and ask him to strip your heart.

> **"A new heart also will I give you, and a new spirit will I put within you: and I will take away the stony heart out of your flesh, and I will give you an heart of flesh. And I will put my spirit within you, and cause you to walk in my statutes, and ye shall keep my judgments, and do them."**
> **(Ezekiel 36:26-27 King James Version)**

If you allow God, He will tell you and show you why love has a lot to do with it. Staying fit with God is important. Your relationship with Him is important. Exercise is very important. Exercise your ability to pray fervently.

> **"Confess your faults one to another, and pray one for another, that ye may be healed. The effectual fervent prayer of a righteous man availeth much."**
> **(James 5:16 King James Version)**

Exercise your ability to study the Word of God.

> **"Study to shew thyself approved unto God, a workman that needeth not to be ashamed, rightly dividing the Word of Truth"**
> **(II Timothy 2:15 King James Version)**

Just as Tina Turner had to connect with her inner self, you need to connect with the Holy Spirit, that should be living on the inside of you so that you can begin exercising love.

> **"The heart is deceitful above all things, and desperately wicked; who can know it?"**
> **(Jeremiah 17:9 King James Version)**

Jeremiah said our hearts are normally deceitful so it is very important we allow the Holy Spirit free reign on the inside of us and teach us how to live, how to love and most of all how to follow Christ in love! What does love have to do with it? It has a lot because Jesus is love! Tell God to strip your heart of every unclean thing that is polluting it and poisoning you. The toxics in our heart is poisoning us and will eventually kill us. Tell God here is my heart God, I give it all to you, strip it and strip it all. Ask God to massage your heart. When those times come, and they will, when the enemy tries to bring all of your hurt back up and all of your disappointments, learn to pull every one of those strongholds down. You are not the victim, you are the victor.

Blind As A Bat

"So why did you have me born? I wish no one had ever laid eyes on me! I wish I'd never lived-a stillborn buried without ever having breathed. Isn't it time to call it quits on my life? Can't you let up, and let me smile just once before I die and am buried, before I'm nailed into my coffin, sealed in the ground. And banished for good to the land of the dead, blind in the final dark?"
(Job 10:18-22 The Message Bible)

In the midst of pain Job was feeling on the inside and outside of his body, he continued to stick up for God and reverence Him. He prayed and spoke with God. Job said he couldn't stand his life. He put all his bitterness on the table. (Chapter 10 of Job).

Job had a conversation with God. He began to tell God to please inform him of what he has done. He wanted to know what Skeleton was in his closet that he had not dealt with. He questioned God about his birth. He wanted to know why did God create Him if He was going to destroy him. Zophar interrupted Job and asked him,

"Do you think you can carry on like this and we'll say nothing?"
Job 11:5 The Message Bible

He told Job to repent and in all of this. Job was adamant about he had done no wrong. He told his friends he was not going to let them, because they were well off, point the finger at him like they had no problems. He told them to let the animals teach them and to put their ear to the ground and listen. True wisdom comes from God and God only.

When we learn to study the Word of God and ask God for wisdom, we will become so wealthy. That is, wealthy of information and discernment. I am not speaking about wealthy of money, even though God can make that happen as well.

Elementary school was tough for me. As I previously told in earlier chapters, I went from being happy to sad to embarrassed to sad again. After my third grade year was completed in Georgia, my sister and I was transferred back to Charlotte, NC because my parents divorced and my maternal grandmother was granted custody of us. I had to begin the fourth grade at a new school with new people again.

While in the fourth grade, I was given an eye test during class and I failed it. I cried and cried because I had never failed anything in school before, so I thought I was going to get in trouble when I got home. My grandmother was not going to help with homework but the rule was you go to school, do what you are supposed to do, and get good grades. That's the only job you have. It's not acceptable to fail anything. After taking the report home to her and she looked at it, she said to me, "Whew you are blind as a bat and you need glasses." I became very upset because I did not want to wear glasses. Glasses would make my life worse than it already was. I was already being called "nerd" and "teacher's pet". Now I was adding "four-eyed". After going to an Optometrist and getting the glasses, the name calling heightened. I was called names like "four-eyed", "Spanish fly" and "nerd". But what sticks out the most is what my grandmother said to me often, "You are blind as a bat".

I never understood what that statement meant so I had to study the bat. We say blind as a bat, but do people really know that bats can really see? Information taken from www.defenders.org. (Basic Facts About Bats). Bats make up ¼ of the mammal species on earth. The #1 myth regarding bats is bats are blind. All bats can see, and many can see very well. "Most fruit-eating bats have large bulging eyes that help them find their way and locate food by sight." Other bats that hunt for insects, they have to rely on their senses to get around in the dark. The reason it seems that they are blind is because they live in dark places and they use echolocation to get around in the dark. We will discuss that in the next chapter. Bats are nocturnal creatures, so they come out at night and sleep during the day.

Our eyes get us into so much trouble, especially if we are not careful. There is evil all around us! If the enemy can get into our eyesight, he has us. We are show me creatures. Everything in the Bible tells us faith should be our eyesight, however we want to see everything with our natural eye.

That is what get us into trouble. He can even cause us to see things that are not there. The enemy can cause us to see illusions. An illusion is defined in dictionary.com as "an idea or something you can see that is not real and something that tricks the eye." The devil will try to make you feel that you are a loser, there's no hope for you, and you will always be in the condition you are in. It is all an illusion. When your eyesight has not been stripped by God, you see things that are not there.

In the back of your eye is a layer of cells called the retina. When light hits the retina it communicates that to the brain. This is what causes you to stay focused on a thing or object. Focus is defined by dictionary.com as "a central point as of attention; to concentrate." When you are focused on a thing, you will have your eyes and mind on that thing, nothing can get you off focus and no one can get you off focus. The problem with us though, is we allow circumstances, problems and distractions to get us off of our "A" game.

Remember, Job was determined, he would not fail God in this task. His friends got him off focus, but after he listened to them and answered each of them, he told them, say what you will, I am taking my case to God myself.

> **"Yes, I've seen all this with my own eyes, heard and understood it with my very own ears. Everything you know, I know, so I'm not taking a backseat to any of you. I'm taking my case straight to God Almighty; I've had it with you-I'm going directly to God. You graffiti my life with lies. You're a bunch of pompous quacks! I wish you'd shut your mouths silence in your only claim to wisdom."**
> **(Job 13:1-5 The Message Bible)**

When we are focused on the things of God, we will not let up. Shut out the negativity around you. Dismiss negative people out of your life. Remember the Law of Attraction. Like attracts like. Job basically told his friends off. He asked them are they not afraid of God? It did not matter to Job what was going on. All he knew was he was not going to take his mind or faith off of God. Even if he died, he was still going to have hope. After talking to his friends, Job went to God with two requests. One was to stop the pain, he couldn't take anymore and the next one was please address him directly. He wanted to know what did he do so badly to deserve all of this. He told God he keeps hoping and waiting for change but nothing is happening. Job was focused on spending time with God.

My nephew Kamari, when he was two years old was a real two year old. He was very, very, very, active, but all he was focused on was football. He wanted a Panther football, Panther football pants (that is what he called them), and a Panther football hat (helmet). No matter what you were talking to him about, he found a way to convert the conversation back to football. So

I decided in my mind, to talk with him and let him know it's more to life besides football. We were trying to broaden his vocabulary and instill education in him. I sat him down and said Kamari I need you to stay focused. I explained what it meant so he could understand it at two. After that, he would say every time he saw me or thought about it, "Auntie I'm focused are you focused?" We all need someone to hold us accountable. That accountability partner should keep us focused on what we need and the things we should be doing. Our problem with that is, we want people to hold us accountable but when they do, we get mad and disconnect from them, so then we connect to people who are going to say yes when we need to and agree with everything we do whether right or wrong. God will also keep you accountable if you allow Him too. Besides God, I have people in all areas of my life to hold me accountable. Having an accountability partner does not mean you have someone that is assigned to stay in your business. But what it means is, that person will keep you lifted up. They will make sure you are on top of your goals and dreams and you are moving towards the end result. I have accountability partners in various areas of my life. I have learned to heed to what they are saying and making sure it line up with my goals and visions from God. I'm never disrespectful, I listen, tell them thank you, take what's mine and dismiss what's not.

It really took some time for me to get that way. I'm usually a focused person, when there is something to do. I allowed circumstances beyond my control to get me off of focus. After graduating High School I went to College and because I allowed circumstances to control my life, I got off focused on my studies and ended up dropping out my sophomore year. After that, my life took a downward spin and everything I got involved in took me further and further away from God which was my first love. I want to go back to a statement that I just said. I allowed things beyond my control to get me off of focus. The question I had to deal with so I could move myself forward was, were they beyond my control or not? Note: Stop blaming others for the decisions that you make. Even if you were coerced, you still made the final decision. As stated in previous chapters I was a good student and got good grades. I was not like many smart students. They were automatically smart. They could hear something or read something and they could retain it. I had to read, study, take notes and study some more. My goal has always been to major in political science or criminal justice and do human service work and become an attorney. All of my dreams went up in smoke when I allowed my focus to leave me. I began living my life according to people. As I write this, I figured out this just stems from my childhood. I always lived my life for people and not for Stella. I turned my life over to Christ at an early age. After all, all I knew was God. So when I went away to college I got a little wild. I tried to keep my foundation by joining the Gospel Choir and going to the Chapel for services, but I still wanted to party and do all the things I could not do while living in my grandmother's home. My life spiraled away from me right before my very own eyes. I began looking for love in all of the wrong places. I wanted someone who would never leave me. My Dad loved me but left me. Then when he came and got me, I felt like he didn't want me because he gave me away again. I didn't understand then, that was a court decision and that he had nothing to do with it. Every guy that I dated used me and left so I began to try to cover my heart because I didn't want to hurt any longer. My focus was so screwed up that I became blind to a lot of things. I have worn a mask, the majority off my life.

When I met my ex-husband I knew things would finally be different. He would take all of this pain away and I could finally be happy. So when little things started happening I would brush it off and say I had to stay in this relationship for the kid's sake. Because of low self-esteem and wanting to be loved, I could not stay focus on me, so things began to really get bad. That is why it was so easy for me to attempt suicide. I had gotten focused on my situation. My mind was cluttered. My heart was broken into many pieces and my eyesight was gone. I left my first love and signed an agreement with Satan himself. Everything and everyone I got involved in took me further and further away. In Revelations 2:1-7, God told the Church of Ephesus they needed to return to their first love. When you are without vision or eyesight you begin to fake the funk. I was faking the funk. Yes I went to Church every Sunday. I know the Word from Genesis 1:1 to Revelations 22:21 very well. I know how to do Church. I been in Church all of my life. I knew how to do Church, but my personal relationship with Christ had diminished. My light had gone out. I was at Church but the Church was not on the inside of me. When that happens it becomes very hard for you to stay focus on the things of God. Just because you are busy in the Church, does not mean the Church is busy on the inside of you. Why does it surprise you, when your vision trips you up over and over again? That is the same reason Job was attacked. God has given the enemy permission to attack you. We look around and we focus on the wrong things, and as we do so, that tends to bring or tear us down. We start to develop our own little pity party. Then these questions begin to plaque our heads. "Why aren't things going my way?" "Why does the Jones' get everything they want?" Why do bad, sinful people get to do so much, and here I'm stuck with nothing?" "Why don't I ever get a break in life?" "Why does bad things always happen to me?" The problem is we often look at things with our natural eyes, rather than our spiritual eyes. We tend to look at things through our physical glasses instead of our very own specialty spiritual glasses subscribed to us by God himself.

"For we walk by faith, not by sight."
(2 Corinthians 5:7 King James Version)

We get off focus because we think we need to see everything and some things God is shielding from us, because if He really showed it to us, it would blow our mind or it could possibly kill us.

So many people have started having Lasik Surgery because they want to improve their eyesight and stop wearing glasses. LASIK stands for Laserinsitukeratomileusis. This is a laser surgery where the surgeon uses a laser underneath a corneal flap to reshape the cornea. This laser is used to treat refractive errors, improve vision, and reduce or eliminate the need for glasses or contact lenses. (Lasik Eye Surgery 12/13/2013 medicinenet.com)

When you can't see, either you are nearsighted, farsighted or blind. When you are nearsighted you are unable to see things far away. You have to squint or bring things closer to you in order to see. I have been diagnosed as nearsighted. When you are far sighted you can't see things up close. Some people are both near and farsighted and they must wear bifocal glasses. When you are blind you cannot see at all. Meaning your eyes and your mind are not working together for the same outcome.

Spiritually we all need LASIK surgery. We must learn to see ourselves the way God see us. We should be around people who see us the way God see us. Our spiritual eyes will allow us to see our supernatural ability. In the natural we see the seen. In the spiritual we see the unseen. When we see Spiritually we see that we are fearfully and wonderfully made in spite of what is going on all around us.

Allow God to put blinders on your eyes so that you will stay focused on the prize which is Eternal Living. If you have ever looked at horse races or a horse being trained, you will see that they put little blinds on the side of the horse's face. The main reason they put blinders on a horse is because it prevents the horses from seeing things that will scare them. It helps them to stay focused on what is in front of them. They won't get distracted by what is on the side of them. This keeps the horses focused on the finish line.

So many things had gotten me off focus that I was considered "walking dead". Why was I walking dead? I was alive physically but on the inside I was DEAD because my focus had gotten off of God. For years I looked good to people on the outside but on the inside I was spiritually dead. I was able to camouflage myself and hide all of that from people. Camouflage defined by American Heritage Dictionary online is "to conceal by the use of disguise or by protective coloring or garments that blend in with the surrounding environment." Most of my life I camouflaged myself. Remember in previous chapters I spoke of wearing a mask. A lizard camouflages itself so that you cannot see it. When it is on a green plant it is green or when it's on something brown, it's brown. My life was just like that. Whatever person I was around or whatever place I was in, I could make myself act like them or my surroundings. I don't know if I was doing it just to fit in or doing it because I was hiding my true feelings of what I had been through. What I did know was, I had done it so long it had become habitual. I was okay as long as I was around people but when I was alone all types of emotions and feelings overtook me. I had actually become a robot. I was able to do anything anyone could ask and do it well but deep down inside I was bleeding. I had become blinded by the darkness. Light blinds many people but I was blinded by the enemy which is darkness. I was so unfocused that many nights from childhood to adulthood, I would cry at night. The enemy began to rejoice because he had succeeded in getting me off of God for real. Superficially I was able to cope but in reality I was dead. I was focused on what I thought was right but it was not what God wanted me focused on.

In the 9th chapter of John we can read the story of the blind man that Jesus mixed mud with spit and put on his eyes. When reading that we take from it, God heals the blind man based on his faith. Actually we can take another approach and say this story is more about the Pharisees who were spiritually blind to God. Many times we are just like the Pharisees. We live in a world where sin has blinded the eyes of even the Christians. Every day we read about or hear about murders, rapes or some other crime.

"Hear, ye deaf; and look, ye blind, that ye may see. Who is blind, but my servant? Or deal, as my messenger that I sent? Who is blind as he that is perfect, and blind as the Lord's servant? Seeing many things, but thou

observes not; opening ears, but he heareth not."
(Isaiah 42: 18-20 King James Version)

The number one reason for spiritual blindness is sin. Sin blinds those who are involved and they don't see their situation as bad.

"Do you see what this means all these pioneers who blazed the way, all these veterans cheering us on? It means we'd better get on with it. Strip down, start running and never quit! No extra spiritual fat, no parasitic sins. Keep your eyes on Jesus, who both began and finished this race we're in. Study how he did it. Because he never lost sight of where he was headed- that exhilarating finish in and with God- he could put up with anything along the way; Cross, shame, whatever. And now he's there, in the place of honor, right alongside God. When you find yourselves flagging in your faith, go over that story again, item by item, that long litany of hostility he plowed through. That will shoot adrenaline into your souls!"
(Hebrews 12:1-3 The Message Bible)

We must stay focused. Being focused is very

important to athletes. If they lose focus of their task they will not be prepared for their opponent. Athletes cannot focus on failure. If they did, they will lose before they even start. Athletes focus on being fit for their game and they also focus on winning. If they can see themselves winning they will do all they can to make their dream a reality. Just like athletes we should not focus on our problems. We should be focusing on a solution for the problem. When your problems seem overwhelming and they are in danger of becoming your focus, remember what Jesus said to the disciples in John 16.

"In this godless world you will continue to experience difficulties. But take heart! I've conquered the world." (John 16:33 The Message Bible)

Please know difficulties, problems, downfalls trials and tribulations will come but it's how you handle it, is what's important. Jesus has already conquered our problems. Problems are not permanent. Hebrews 3:1 tell us to focus on Him above. If we focus on Him then we do not have time to focus on other people, problems, or circumstances or the things around us.

I had to go through my very own Damascus experience in order for my eyes to be stripped to see like Him and to see what He would have for me to see. The first Damascus Experience was experienced by Saul whom after his eyesight was stripped he became Paul. Paul, then Saul, was a persistent enemy and persecutor of the Christian Church, after it was founded in Jerusalem by the Holy Spirit. He thought he was doing the right thing. So many times we are doing things and we think it is right but in all actuality it is not. Read the story of Saul/Paul in Acts 9. Saul was on his way to Damascus when he was struck blind by a bright light. A voice spoke to Saul letting him know that Jesus was speaking to him and he was persecuting Him. Saul was blind for 3 days, neither eating nor drinking, before God returned his sight to him by using a man named Ananias. Saul was baptized and began really living for Christ. Saul's name was changed to Paul. His Damascus Road Experience was a life changing experience for him because he had to be stripped by his lover before he could be transformed.

My Damascus Road Experience is not as drastic as Paul's experience by getting knocked off of a horse and blinded but he had to take scales off of my eyes in order for me to see clearly. I saw everything negatively. I could see someone being blessed but could not see myself being blessed. I could see God elevating someone else but never saw Him elevating me. I knew God could bless. I knew God could deliver. I knew God could heal. I just never expected him to do any of that for me. I remember hearing a song by Pastor Marvin Winans entitled, "Draw Me Close To Thee/Thy Will Be Done" In the song he says I seen you Work in others and I want you to work in me. I was that person that saw God working but never saw Him working through me. It was not until I really had to seek God for a healing for my daughter that I really had to see beyond the now and trust God. It was not until I was in my state of depression and losing my mind that I really had to see beyond what I was going through and trust in God. It was not until I was stripped of everything physically, emotionally, mentally and spiritually that I had to see beyond the stripping and still trust God.

What is your Damascus Road Experience? God can open your eyes. He is able to do exceedingly and abundantly beyond all we could ever ask or think. God is able to do it for us. We must denounce our own eyesight and ask God to order our eyesight to see beyond the now and see what is going to be.

Focusing can be difficult, but you have to do whatever you have to do to stay focus. If you have to cut yourself free from some people to stop the distractions when they first come then do that. Change some numbers and change some addresses. Delete some people off facebook, twitter, Instagram, periscope, etc. You must do those things to stay focused on the things of God. Staying focused sets us free from other people's expectations and keep us free to do what God has purposed for us to do.

"No, Christian brothers, I do not have that life yet. But I do know one thing. I forget everything that is behind me and look forward to that which is ahead of me. My eyes are on the crown. I want to win the race and get the crown of God's call from Heaven through Christ Jesus." (Philippians 3:13-14 New Living Translation Version)

It does not matter if you have gotten off focus this year. What matters is if you have breath in your body then you have been given another opportunity to focus on the things of God and let Him handle those other things. It took me a long time to learn that and yes I made mistake after mistake and yes I was saved, sanctified, Holy Ghost filled and preaching the Word of God but when I came into the knowledge of the truth, I had to change some things. It takes time and practice and most of all it takes God. Allow God to spit on the ground and make a mud pie and put on your eyes so that you will be healed from your blindness.

The Tornado

"Eliphaz of Teman spoke a second time: 'If you were truly wise, would you sound so much like a windbag, belching hot air? Would you talk nonsense in the middle of a serious argument, babbling baloney? Look at you! You trivialize religion, turn spiritual conversation into empty gossip. It's your sin that taught you to talk this way. You chose an education in fraud. Your own words have exposed your guilt. It's nothing I've said- you've incriminated yourself.'"
(Job 15:1-6 The Message Bible)

Job still didn't give up on God. After he prayed to God, his friend Eliphaz spoke again. This time his attack came harsher than the first. He told Job to stop talking nonsense. He has turned the things of the Spirit into gossip. He told him he is talking the way he is, because of his sin. He asked Job was he around when God created the world and why do he think he knows everything? After Eliphaz finished telling Job off in Job chapter 15, Job retaliated in Chapter 16.

> **"When I speak up, I feel no better;**
> **if I say nothing, that doesn't help either.**
> **I feel worn down."**
> **(Job 16:6 The Message Bible)**

Job told Eliphaz he was tired of his noise. Job began talking to God again. He told God and his friends that his prayers were sincere. Everything that proceeded out of his mouth was truth. He asked God whatever he had done please tell him. He told God he is the talk of the town. Everyone was gossiping about him. Bildad spoke up and tried to attack Job again. He asked Job why was he treating his friends like that. He began to ridicule Job. Job again turned and asked Bildad how long were they going to be harassing him? He asked them why are they questioning him, God is who they should be talking too. Everyone despised Job, all of his family, servants, friends and enemies. He asked his friends why are they being so hard on him, God is already doing that.

Our tongue should be used to encourage, help, build up and witness. Our tongue can be just like a tornado. Tornado is defined in Dictionary.com as "a violent outburst, as of emotion or activity." Our tongue can really live up to that definition. When we speak hastily or when we speak unthoughtfully or even when we speak thoughtfully but we say the wrong thing, the tongue produces disastrous results. If you wish to love and enjoy life, the very first thing you must do is stop your tongue. Few tongues are disciplined and controlled. Our tongue get us into a whole lot of trouble. Why? Because we don't think before we speak. The tongue is a dangerous weapon. It reacts, attacks, defend, teases, poisons, cuts, hurts, scolds, praises and degrades.

The tongue poses the greatest threat to the Kingdom of God. James 3:1-12 talks about taming the tongue. But verse 2 tells us if anyone is never at fault in what he says, he is a perfect man and that person is able to keep his entire body in check. There is no perfect person, so all of us at some time or another, things will get the best of us. Whatever is in our heart will flow out of our mouth. When we get upset we tend to say things we don't even mean. Our tongue starts fires.

"There is that speaketh like the piercings of a sword: but the tongue of the wise is health."
(Proverbs 12:18 King James Version)

Reckless words pierce like a sword, but the tongue of the wise brings healing. Tongues are toxic.

> **"For the Scriptures say, If you want to enjoy life and see many happy days, keep your tongue from speaking evil and your lips from telling lies."**
> **(I Peter 3:10 New Living Translation)**

An evil tongue is a tongue that curses, backbites, refuses instruction, retaliates and gossip among a few. The Word of God teaches us to refrain from that and live an enjoyable and happy life.

The tongue is comprised of 8 muscles, membranes and nerves. The tongue grows to be about 10 cm or 4 inches long. The tongue is there so we may chew, taste, swallow and speak. Even though the tongue is small it carries a lot of weight.

> **"Death and life are in the power of the tongue and those who love it will eat its fruit."**
> **(Proverbs 18:21 New King James Version)**

"Words kill, words give life, they're either poison or fruit

you choose"
(Proverbs 18:21 The Message Bible Version)

What we say effects and affects every part of our lives. Many times we open our mouth and say things that get us in trouble. Some things we have said has come back to haunt us and hurt us. There is power in what you say. So you must be careful of what you say. We can speak and bring life and resurrection to something that seemed to have died and been removed from our life. You may say 'I don't feel well or I am sick' and your body begins to respond to that affirmation. There are many times we have brought things on our self because of what we have said. On the flip side of that we allow people to speak over us in a negative way. You may have left the house feeling well and expecting a great day. As soon as you get to work, someone else takes one look at you and say you look like you don't feel well. Someone else come up to you and ask you 'are you feeling okay today, you look funny?' Someone else walk up to you and ask you 'what's wrong, you don't look good today?' Before you know it you are saying "I don't feel well!"

I was not only a product of negative thinking, but I was a product of negative speaking. In order for me to begin walking into my destiny, my thinking and my speaking had to line up to the Word of God. The Scripture tells us that praises and curses don't come out of the same mouth. Cursing is not just profane language that you may speak or as some say those four letter words. Cursing is defined by dictionary.com as, "to wish or invoke evil, calamity, injury or destruction upon; to swear at; to blaspheme; to afflict with great evil." Many times we curse without even using profanity. When we speak down over our lives, we are cursing ourselves. Every time you open your mouth and confess that the enemy has really got you down, you have given him information to use against you.

Be careful when you speak judgment on somebody.

**"Judge not, and ye shall not be judged; condemn not, and ye shall not be condemned; forgive and ye shall be forgiven; Give, and it shall be given unto you, good measure, pressed down and shaken together, and running over, shall men give unto your bosom. For with the same measure that ye mete withal it shall be measured to you again."
(Luke 6:37-38 King James Version)**

When you are critical and very judgmental you bring all of that back on you.

In Chapter 1, I mentioned you have to think about what you are thinking about. In this chapter I must take it a little further and say you must begin to think about what you are going to say before you say it. If we think about what we say before we speak, we would be living in a better world. Life and death is in the power of your tongue. Our tongue will get out of control very easily. It causes things around us to get out of control.

I had to learn how to control my tongue. It took a while for me to get it. If I would have gotten it the first time I would not be writing this chapter over in book two. With my mouth I never intended to hurt anyone intentionally. That is not in my character. I have always been careful in choosing my words so that I would not hurt anyone's feelings, no matter what they said or did to me. So how was I rude with my tongue? I was not cautious on what I said to myself or about myself.

Sometimes things we speak is good and of God but God must direct you when to speak and when not to speak. You must be in the perfect timing of God. God shows many of you visions and dreams. He may show you the correct path or journey to your destiny. You must keep your mouth closed and not tell a soul until God directs you when to speak and what to say. You speaking prematurely may cause havoc, jealousy or chaos as soon as it comes out of your mouth.

If you speak prematurely before God releases you, it will cause the enemy to throw you off course. The story of Joseph is told in Genesis 37-50. Joseph's brothers were already jealous of him because they felt their father favored Joseph out of all the sons. In the 37th chapter of Genesis, Joseph had a vision from God. In the vision he and his brothers were binding sheaves of grain out in the field. Joseph told them that his sheaf rose and stood upright, while their sheaves gathered around his shaves and bowed down to it. They grew a dislike and hatred against their brother. Why? Because Joseph was telling them he would be great and they would have to bow down to him one day. Even though Joseph may not have meant to tell them in a bragging way, they took it as such. Joseph was so excited he just couldn't keep his mouth closed. Sometimes we tell things before God is ready to release. In Psalm 119:113 David asks God to order his steps and we should be asking God to order our tongues.

I had to be stripped of my mouth, tongue and speech. Like Joseph I would prematurely share with people visions and or prophecies from God. I thought they had my best interest in mind. However what I shared became a joke and then became gossip around town. The devil got in the midst and began to throw distractions and daggers in the way. If I confessed then what I confess much now, I would have quoted:

"No weapon that is formed against thee shall prosper; and every tongue that shall rise against thee in judgment thou shalt condemn. This is the heritage of the servants of the Lord and their righteousness is of me, saith the Lord."
(Isaiah 54:17 King James Version)

We quote that Scripture often but have we ever dissected it to really understand it's meaning? This verse means to me; it does not matter how many attacks I endure, they won't be successful. The attacks come because God gave the enemy permission to attack but he cannot touch our soul. Many of those attacks are not our fault. It is because God know that we will not forsake Him and turn on Him.

If I would have had control over my mouth, some things I went through would not have come my way. And if it had come, I would have known how to strategically handle it.

"I tell you, on the day of judgment people will give account for every careless word they speak." (Matthew 12:36 English Standard Version)

I had to repent again. If you allow God to strip your heart, your tongue will follow.

"Jesus replied, 'You too? Are you being stupid? Don't you know that anything that is swallowed works its way through the intestines and is finally defecated? But what comes out of the mouth gets its start in the heart. It's from the heart that we vomit up evil arguments, murders, adulteries, fornications, thefts, lies, and

cussing. That's what pollutes. Eating or not eating certain foods, washing or not washing your hand- that's neither here or there. Healing the people.'"
(Matthew 15: 16-20 The Message Bible)

The reason I had to be stripped of my heart was because of what was coming out of my mouth. Remember the Scripture 'out of your heart flows issues! Hurt people, hurt people. When you have been hurt physically, emotionally, mentally, verbally, or spiritually, you will intentionally or non-intentionally hurt someone else unless you have healed totally. It is important that you are very careful of the Words that come out of your mouth. This is one reason that I know that I should not have gotten married when I did. I was hurt, abused, misused and was not ready for another relationship but when you hear the statement that 'a piece of a man is better than no man' most of your life, it becomes embedded in you. I was messed up and I took all of that mess into a relationship and tried to be happy.

Discipline is very important when it comes to controlling your tongue. Dictionary.com defines discipline as "training to act in accordance with rules; activity, exercise, or a regiment that develops or improves a skill." You must practice speaking positive things before you speak.

Professionals state anything that you do between 21 and 30 days continuously becomes a habit. I stated early that I was stripped of my tongue. Was it an easy process? No! I have no problem in humbling myself. I also have no problem in admitting that I am not always right. What I do have to work on though is, when I am right, I must figure out a better way to say it before it comes out of my mouth. I had to learn how to use the words, kindness, forgiveness and grace. By being stripped of my mouth, I had to learn to speak less. I must also refuse to listen to gossip and slander about others. The hardest thing for me was to bring my thought pattern under the control of the Holy

Spirit. When you allow the Holy Spirit to lead and guide you, your thought pattern changes, your speech changes and your negativity becomes positivity.

Watch the words you speak. Your words will bring life or your words will bring death. There is no other alternative. We can experience an overflow of blessings by the words we speak or we can speak an overflow of curses by the words we speak. I remember a chant we use to say when I was a little girl. We use to say "Sticks and stones may break my bones, but words will never hurt me." I don't even know why we said that because that is an untrue statement. Words hurt and sometimes hurts to a point of a non-repairable damage. Broken bones can heal over time. Words that are spoken over us can send us into a deep depression. I was a "depressaholic". I know that is not a word, but that is where I was. Depression is defined as "the act of lowering something or pressing something down; a sunken place or hollow on a surface." Because I heard the words, "you are worthless, and will never amount to anything" "you are just like your mother" "you are just like your father" all of the time, it began to become residue in my life. What I never understood was what did being like my parents have anything to do with it. I look like my mother (twins) and look like my father (twins). Some things are DNA passed down and it is how I choose to deal with it that will determine the outcome. Verbal abuse begins to become residue for you, if you don't deal with it. The words we speak can also effect the world around us. What we say, and how we communicate with each other has lasting results. Words are significant. The book of James in the Bible tell us our words can direct us and others in life. Our words have control over which way our life will go. Words will also determine your destiny. Our tongue is small and because it is so small, we count it out as insignificant. But the tongue is very powerful.

> **"rash language cuts and maims, but there is healing in the words of the wise."**
> **(Proverbs 12:18 The Message Bible)**

> **"If you want to stay out of trouble be careful what you say."**
> **(Proverbs 21:23 The Message Bible)**

We must allow God to transform our tongue to speak wisdom. Let God strip your tongue so that your words will have the power to heal. Start being positive. Think before you speak. Write down affirmations and affix them to a place you frequent daily. Repeat those affirmations till they become a part of you. You need to know what to say and when to say it. Don't let your tongue destroy you like a tornado will do when it hits. Ask God to help you daily.

> **"Set a guard over my mouth, O Lord; keep watch over the door of my lips."**
> **(Psalm 141:3 New King James Version)**

A prayer that we should get into the habit of praying daily is "God muzzle my mouth and guard my lips. Help me not to be critical. Help me not to be judgmental and help me to watch my words."

"He that keepeth his mouth, keepeth his life; But he that openeth wide his lips shall have destruction. (Proverbs 13:3 King James Version)

Hear No Evil

"Look at me- I shout, 'Murder'! and I'm ignored; I call for help and no one bothers to stop."
(Job 19:7 The Message Bible)

Job's friends continued to harass him about repenting, so that all the trouble and heartache would stop for him. Job said, "I'm crying out for help but no one is listening to me." Job also said, "my family is gone and the relatives I have left won't even come around me." He told his friends God is already disciplining him, he don't need it from his friends as well. He told them even though all of this is happening to him, he still know, there is a God! God is the only one that can give Job his life back. Job said even though all of this has happened, he still longs for the day that he will see God face to face. Job begged his friends to stop worrying about Him and worry about themselves because God is coming to judge individually and not collectively.

Zorphar got mad and told Job, "I can't believe what I am hearing." He told him to remember the story of Adam and Eve, wicked one and wicked things are short lived. Evil ones look like they may be on top of the world but it will soon be cut off. Job stopped Zophar and told him to listen to him. He told him they can just be quiet because he was not complaining to them, he was complaining to God, because God is not speaking to him. All the evil in the world is going on and God is silent to Him.

Eliphaz spoke up again. He said no one is strong enough to give God help. He asked Job if he was righteous would God notice? He also asked Job if he was perfect would God applaud him and did he think God cared about his purity that he is disciplined. Job said NO! Eliphaz told Job because he was a first class failure and his sins are endless, he is getting first class discipline because of his sins. He told Job he was wealthy and did not help anybody and now he has to deal with all of that. Job replied to Eliphaz that his complaint to God is legit because everything they are saying is wrong. He told him he has done nothing to deserve all of this. He told them he obeyed everything from God, but

God can do what He wants to do because this is his world.

Bildad decides to attack Job for the third time. He told Job, God is sovereign. He told Job that he might as well give it up no one can stand up to God. God is too majestic and powerful. Job tells Bildad he has really been help to a helpless man and then he had the nerve to talk about him. He told his friends, God may have taken away his rights, God may have made him unhappy, but as long as he lives, he will not speak evil nor will he lie. He told them till he die he will keep crying out that he is innocent. He told his friends he will never denounce God so why are they having this useless conversation?

We must be very careful of what we allow into the gates of our ears. Job stood his ground, however many of us listen to things and we are not strong enough to hold our own and rebuke the enemy as the enemy approaches us with all of that nonsense.

> **"Then He said to them, take heed what you hear. With the same measure you use, it will be measured to you; and to you who hear, more will be given. For whoever has, to him more will be given; but whoever does not have, even what he has will be taken away from him."**
> **(Mark 4:24-25 King James Version)**

If someone is saying something and we know without a shadow of a doubt, it is damaging to our spirit or it is merely a distraction then you must immediately shut it down. What goes in your ears goes directly into your heart.

> **"And God saw that the wickedness of man was great in the earth, and that every imagining of the thoughts of his heart was only evil continually."**
> **(Genesis 6:5 King James Version)**

When I was a little girl I remember playing a game with my aunts. We would put our hands over our eyes, ears and lips and say see no evil, hear no evil and speak no evil. The Body of Christ need to go back to the

Preschool games we use to play. They make sense and cause you to think. They taught me to be careful in what I say. Be careful with what I listen to, and be careful with what I watch or look at. Somewhere down the line I forgot all about my foundation. If you are built on a solid foundation, when you stray away you won't stray away long.

"Train up a child in the way he should go and when he is old, he will not depart from it."
(Proverbs 22:6 King James Version)

I was raised with a good foundation. I can only blame myself for the things that happen throughout my life. I made my own decisions. Stop blaming others for your downfall, you had a lot to do with it.

Heed is defined by Merriam-Webster dictionary as "pay attention, listen carefully, be careful, be on guard, and watch over." With our lips we say we are taking heed to the things around us but when trials and tribulations come it is a different story.

Things we hear can be detrimental to our own faith. I remember praying and because I felt like God was not answering my prayers, I started studying other religions and listening to other religions and began wondering if there really was a God. Don't judge me. It's somebody reading this right now who has wondered the same thing before, you just did not voice it. I had to know for myself that there is a God. I had to know for myself and not what my grandparents were saying to me that God was hearing my prayers. I had to experience God for myself. I found out that God was hearing my prayers and He was answering my Prayers. He just was not answering them like I wanted him too. In the midst of my stripping God had to remind me of what the Word of God says.

"Without faith it's impossible to please Him."
Hebrews 11:6 (KJV)

I had to learn throughout all I was going

through I had to strengthen my faith.

We learned in the chapter, "What's Love Got To Do With It, " that important things come from the heart. We must first watch what we hear because what we hear can effect and affect are faith. After it infiltrate our faith it get in our heart and then begin to do damage. Remember Proverbs 4:23 says out of our heart flows issues of life. My hearing had to be stripped because I allowed any and everything to enter my ears and go straight to my spirit. Because I was not careful of what I was listening to, depression, low self-esteem, hatred, jealousy, self-centeredness, lack of trust all seeped into me and caused my life to take a spiral downward turn. When I allowed God to take control of my life and totally do a strip search on me, my ears were unstopped and I was able to hear clearly and change the way I did things. It was not an overnight process for me and still today I have to cast down things so it won't take root on the inside of me.

In the "Blind As A Bat" chapter we talked about bats. But I'm here to tell you that bats also have a high sense of hearing. Bats do not rely on their sense of sight at night. At night they rely on their sense of hearing. Bats make rapid high pitched squeaks. These squeaks are called ultrasounds. These ultrasounds are too high for most people to hear. If these sounds hit something, they bounce back. When they bounce back the bats hear the echo and they can tell where the object is. This technique is called echolocation. Our hearing should be just like that. We should bounce what we hear off in our minds and if it goes against the Word of God or the Word of Knowledge that you know, then don't speak it.

In the book of Revelations, Jesus told the 7 churches 7 times "he that hath an ear, hear what the Spirit has to say to the churches". The Holy Spirit was speaking to God's people. He is still talking and waiting for us to hear his voice. For those who listen and obey, they are about to move forward into the greatest outpouring of God's spirit that the world has ever known. They just have to hear what the Spirit was saying. Some of us have so much going on in our lives that when God speak to us we don't hear him. Jesus tell us in John 10:27 that His sheep know His voice. When you are stripped of your hearing all factors begin to line up right. We are what we eat. We are what we think. We are what we hear. The most crucial problem we all face when it comes to hearing God is the motive of our own hearts. We can know our Bible backwards and forwards. We can be so spiritual but if the primary pursuit of our heart is not right we will have trouble hearing the voice of God. We will have trouble getting clear direction for our lives.

We as Christians are very quick to say, we love God and want to obey Him. We want to be like Isaiah and say 'Here Am I Lord!' God often speak but we don't listen. In Jeremiah 26:1-8 we find the people of Judah in trouble.

God gave them a warning. All God wanted was the people to listen and obey. They heard Prophet Jeremiah's warning but they didn't listen. Listening and hearing are two different things. To hear is defined as "to perceive with the ear the sound made by someone or something." To listen is defined as "give one's attention to a sound." By these definitions listening to God is far more than hearing. Hearing is the starting point of where we receive God's word. We can't listen if we can't hear, God.

There are times in our life when we experience a season of dryness in our soul, because God is trying to speak something to us and we are not really listening and we are being disobedient. There are many different ways that we don't hear God. A circumstantial factor will impact our ability to hear. God can speak to us through parables in order to get our attention. Jeremiah couldn't hear what God was saying, until he saw the marring of the clay and the remaking of the clay. Sometimes we need to be in a physical location to hear from God. When we are running from one place to the next it causes chaos and we cannot really hear what God is trying to say to us. Make a place in your home where you consistently spend time with God. You must not always be the one talking when you go to God. God had to really get my attention. I was always the one doing the talking, but never waiting for God to speak back. I pray, get up and go about my business. God was wanting to speak to me, but my ears were stopped up. I could not obey the voice of God because I was not listening to God.

"In your seed all the nations of the earth shall be blessed, because you have obeyed my voice." (Genesis 22:18 New King James Version)

Many of my blessings were in the "hold up" stage because I was not obeying the voice of God. There are many things God has equipped, called and elected me, but my disobedience stopped me from being all God intended me to be.

> **"But only if you listen obediently to God, your God, and keep the commandments and regulations written on this Book of Revelation. Nothing halfhearted here; you must return to God, your God, totally, heart and soul, holding nothing back. This commandment that I'm commanding you today isn't too much for you, it's not out of your reach. It's not on a high mountain-you don't have to get mountaineers to climb the peak and bring it down to your level and explain it before you can live it. And it's not across the ocean-you don't have to send sailors out to get it, bring it back, and then explain it before you can live it. No. The Word is right here and now as near as the tongue in your mouth, as near as the heart in your chest. Just do it!"**
> **(Deuteronomy 30:10-14 The Message Bible)**

God is requesting our obedience. The only way to be obedient, you must be able to hear and listen to the instructions given by God.

> **"But my people would not heed My voice, And Israel would have none of Me. So I gave them over to their**

own stubborn heart, to walk in their own counsels. Oh, that My people would listen to Me. That Israel would walk in My ways!"
(Psalm 81:11-13 King James Version)

There were many times that I felt like I was just wandering and God had taken his hands off of me because I was not doing, what he was expecting me to do. It was not until I made up in my mind, changed my heart, changed my speech, changed how I looked at things, then God began to open up blessings for me.

When we are stripped of our hearing we have augmented ears. Augmented ears is a human enhancement concept that explores the idea of augmented hearing senses. Augmented ears is when you are able to hear different frequencies of sound. It helps you to filter all unwanted noise away and to compose a personal sound by picking one frequency or combining two frequencies. When your ears are augmented in the spirit you are able to filter out all things that are not like God. You are able to discern and hear God for yourself. God is a stripper and when you allow him to really strip you, you will hear no evil. You will block all things out that should not enter and only allow the things to enter your Spirit that will build you and bring you out.

Wisdom Is Key

"And unto man he said, Behold the fear of the Lord, that is wisdom; and to depart from evil is understanding. (Job 28:28 King James Version)

Job had to continue to defend himself. Then he turned it back and asked where will they find wisdom and insight. He told his so called friends only God knows the way of wisdom and where to find it. God knows everything. He began to tell his friends he misses when God took good care of him. God use to protect his home. He was respected by old and young in town. When he spoke everyone listened to him. He was known for helping people in trouble and standing up for those that were having a rough time. Job told them he was a leader and everyone followed him. But now the tables has changed, he is now the one everyone is joking on, mistreating, mocking and abusing. He said he continues to cry out to God but God is not answering. Job then asked his friends what should he expect from God? Does not God reward calamity with the wicked? Does God not pay attention to the way he lives their life? He asked has his entire life been lived incorrectly?

Because Job did not give in to his friends they didn't know what else to say. Elihu got very angry. He told Job he cannot compare his righteousness to the righteousness of God. He also got mad at Job's 3 friends for not winning against Job. He told them he was young and they should have wisdom and experience. He asked Job to please listen to Him. He told Job he cannot compare God to a human. God will answer people. Many times things happen in our life to get our attention. He also told Job, God will get the attention He really wants through pain. He told Job he messed up in his life but God stepped in and saved him from death. God is the one that will pull you out of destruction. Elihu told Job he was there to teach him the basics of wisdom.

Elihu addressed all of them by saying, "we have all heard what Job has said but how can you condemn God? Does God play favorites with the rich and famous and slight the poor? Isn't God equal to everyone?"

Elihu told them if God is silent, so what. God is always there ruling. He asked Job what is it going to hurt him to confess his sins to God, nobody is perfect. He also told him to tell God to teach him to see what he still does not see. Elihu told Job you cannot be wishy washy. One minute Job said he was perfectly innocent before God. And then the next minute Job said It doesn't make a bit of difference whether he sinned or not. He told Job don't let the riches he had, mislead him. God is powerful and He is the best teacher there is. God is infinite even in the midst of trouble. No one can escape from God.

> **"My people are destroyed for lack of knowledge; because thou hast rejected knowledge, I will also reject thee, that thou shalt be no priest to me; seeing thou hast forgotten the law of thy God, I will also forget they children."**
> **(Hosea 4:6 King James Version)**

I personally had to be stripped of my own knowledge. That may sound crazy to you, but I am a professional student. I don't mind reading. I don't mind studying. I don't mind unlocking the mysteries of the Word of God. Even through all of that I was dying for the lack of knowledge. You may know the Word of God and you may be able to quote the Scriptures from Genesis 1:1 through Revelations 22:21 verbatim, but without the ability to apply it to your life makes your life void of knowledge. That is where Stella Hall was. I was able to quote and tell you what the Word said but unable to apply it to my very own life. I could not apply the Word to my situations. I could not apply the Word to my trial and tribulations. I could not understand how to make the Word work for me.

Earlier in the book I told you how I dealt with things. I would put on a mask when I wanted to hide from a situation. I need to be a bit candied now because I don't want anyone reading this to die because of the lack of knowledge.

My state of depression did not just happen

all of a sudden. It started back when I was a little girl. If I could say so, I would probably pinpoint it all the way back before I was conceived. Depression is a disease and it can also be hereditary. Depression comes from somewhere and if you don't cut it off at the root, it will continue to come back. When you plant flowers in a garden and you go back after a while to get the weeds out, if you don't pull the weeds up from root, they will continue to come back. That is exactly what happened to me. EHealthmd.com defines depression as "a disorder that involves feelings of sadness lasting for two weeks or longer, often accompanied by a loss of interest in life, hopelessness, and decreased energy. Such distressing feelings can affect one's ability to perform the usual tasks and activities of daily living. Depression affects the mind, but this doesn't mean it's all in your head! Depression is a medical illness linked to changes in the biochemistry of the brain. Depression is not a weakness of character. Being depressed does not mean that a person is inadequate. It means the person has a medical illness that is just as real as diabetes, ulcers, cancer, or Hiv/Aids. Like other medical disorders, clinical depression should not be ignored or dismissed. A clinically depressed person cannot simply 'snap out of it' any more than a person with an ulcer could simply will it away." It took me a very long time to realize that I had a disorder called depression and I had it while I was a child. Because of depression I held feelings in on the inside of me. I allowed people to do or say whatever they wanted to do or say to me. I began looking for love in all of the wrong places and people because I did not know how to love myself. During family gatherings you may find me in the middle of the crowd laughing and talking with people or you would find me in a corner somewhere either, just sitting and pretending I was elsewhere or you would find me in a corner by myself with a book reading or writing.

Depression is the common cold of our emotions. If we want to experience victorious living we have to learn how to deal with depression. Elijah in the Bible had to deal with depression. Elijah was living during the days of King Ahab and Queen Jezebel. Elijah was chosen by God to challenge the King and the prophets of Baal and to call the nation back from apostasy. Apostasy is defined as abandonment of one's religious faith, a political party, one's principles, or a cause. Elijah had a contest on Mt. Carmel between Baal and the Spirit of God. Even thou Elijah was victorious Elijah sunk into depression. He sat up under a juniper tree and asked God to take his life.

Many times we are exhausted, overwhelmed, and depressed with no apparent way to get out of our circumstances. Sometimes that depression can sink so low it may seem as if the only way out is to take your life. You are not alone in your struggle even though it seems that way most of the time. I told you previously that I attempted suicide. I wanted my life to end. I could not handle the many obstacles and hurdles. My life was in a whirlwind and I wanted it to stop and did not know I had the authority to speak to the whirlwind and command it to stop. Nothing was going right for me. Trials and tribulations were coming left and right and I felt as though no one understood what I was going through. My life as a wife and mother, I felt like I was more of a burden than a help. It is all good and great to throw Scriptures at people but if you have not walked in their shoes and don't have a testimony of how God brought you through that situation, it is a little hard for you to help someone. I knew the Word of God but during that time I could not even pull the Word out of me to help myself. I was already dead spiritually and wanted to be dead physically. The problem was no one could help me out of my situation. The only out I could think of was to end it all and no one would have to deal with me or hear my problems any longer. I had a lack of wisdom and knowledge of how to try the Spirit by the Spirit for my own life. After pulling the trigger of the gun and nothing happened, the Holy Spirit prompt me to look on the bed and Antonio (6), BrayAnna (3) and DeJa (1) was lying on the bed asleep. I heard the Spirit say who is going to take care of them. I was not thinking I would be burdening others because someone would have to take my responsibility of raising my kids. The Lord said who will mature them and who would train them. I needed help and I needed immediate help. I called my Pastor and Co-Pastor and they told me to meet them at the Church. When they got there I was already laying at the altar. I don't even remember them coming in, I just remember being wrapped in their arms and them praying and toiling with me that night. I did not leave till I felt the release of Satan! After that night things got better and brighter for me. My assumption was I was finally delivered from depression. Remember I said if you do not cut things at the root it will come back to haunt you again. When you assume it makes an *ass* u * me.

April 13, 2005, the nurse at the Elementary School Bray'Anna (my oldest daughter, second born) attended called me. She told me that Bray'Anna needed to see a doctor because every day she was getting sick. I remember telling Nurse Flo, nothing was wrong with her. She may have been getting sick in school but she was making herself sick because she didn't like school and she was fine when she got home. Nurse Flo stated she was putting in her records that Bray'Anna could not return to school unless she had a doctor's excuse clearing her to return to school. I must admit I was really annoyed but I made Bray'Anna a doctor's appointment for Thursday, April 14, 2005. We went to Bray'Anna's Dr. appointment.

After Dr. Elkin's examined her and took some blood. He said, "Ms. Reid, it looks as though your daughter is suffering with Juvenile Diabetes. We are not going to prescribe anything till the labs come back. The nurse will call you tomorrow with what medication we will prescribe." He wrote a note for Bray'Anna to return to school. She did not feel like going to school, so we went home. All that day I felt a burning in the pit of my stomach and did not know why. You know that feeling you get when you know something devastating is about to happen in your life? The next day Dr. Elkins called me directly. He said, "Ms. Reid I have good news and I have some bad news." I told him to give me the good news first. He then precedes to tell me Bray'Anna did not have Juvenile Diabetes. I was a bit relieved, but still tensed because I did not know what the bad news was. He then preceded to tell me that Bray'Anna has glomerulonephritis. (Right that was Greek to me as well). I of course asked him what did that mean. He stated it is the same as Chronic Renal Failure. Both of her kidneys were beginning to go out. I was speechless. I did not know what to say. I heard him call my name but I could not answer. Finally I was able to ask what do we do now? He then said "I will call you back, if I can get her a specialty appointment she will be okay. If I can't, I am going to admit her in the hospital. She needs attention now!" I was dumbfounded. All types of thoughts were entering into my head. I was still holding the phone in my hand when it rang. It was Dr. Elkins saying he did not have to admit her. He was able to get her an appointment on Monday morning, April 18, 2005 at the Carolinas Medical Center Children's Specialty Center.

Never say never! I said I would never go back to that state of depression that I found myself in before. Immediately, I began to feel a heaviness surround me. All kinds of thoughts began filling my head. I felt so numb and all I can hear in my head was because of your sins your daughter is going to die. I was so discombobulated. This was the longest weekend of my life. When we went to meet the Specialty Doctors or Nephrologist I did not know what to expect but they made our first meeting a very memorable one. We were told she needed to go on dialysis, however they were going to try and wait till the end of her fourth grade school year. She was able to go back to school. Our next appointment was two weeks later which was the first week in May. We went back as scheduled but her lab reports showed she needed to go on dialysis immediately. After talking with the school they stated she was okay and would be promoted to the fifth grade. Surgery to place her on peritoneal dialysis was scheduled.

I am normally a Radical Praiser but I found it very hard to praise God. The thank you Jesus that I had, turned into a "Why God are you doing this to me?" I was perishing for the lack of knowledge that I really did have on the inside of me. When I told those connected to me what was going on they immediately wanted to pray. Honestly, I did not want to pray! I wanted someone to wake me up, so that I could stop this nightmare.

Why did I feel my depression coming back? Because I did not cut it off at the root. All of the thoughts I previously had was coming back and there was nothing that I could do. Everyone was calling me and telling me God will make away. Do you think I really wanted to hear that? No I did not! I was losing my mind again and no one could see that. I was a walking zombie. I was very experienced in wearing a mask. I was walking around, helping my daughter to cope with her new disability, working a full time job, and ministering on top of all the other duties I had at Church and was literally dying. All of my Word that I could give to everyone else had left me, so I thought. After all those many years, I still could not apply the Word to my situation. Because I was perishing, my daughter was getting sicker and sicker and I thought there was nothing that I could do about it.

November 27, 2005, I heard a sermon entitled "Power of Words and Thoughts". I sat there and watched it on television and I felt like he was talking directly to me and there was no one around. In that sermon God spoke directly to me. God told me things would get better but I must let everything I have learned and been taught go out of the window. In other words God was saying to me, let him strip me of "my knowledge and wisdom" and let him give me "his knowledge and wisdom". After that sermon and that encounter with God I really repented and began speaking life over my life, life over my children and everything around us. That experience with God transformed my life. Because of my words, the enemy tried to make me out of a liar.

When I took Bray'Anna to the doctor

December 2005, the doctor stated if we do not get a transplant or a miracle happens quickly, Bray'Anna would not be with us long. I knew I was finally delivered of that state of depression because I immediately went into prayer and began commanding miracles to happen over my daughter.

To summarize a long journey for us, on January 29, 2006 at 3:20am, I got a phone call from Carolinas Healthcare Nephrology Department stating they had a kidney from an accident and it looked favorable that Bray'Anna can receive it. This was a true miracle. December 2005, Bray'Anna was well over 200 on the donor list and her blood type is common so by statistics it should have taken over 3 years for her name to hit #1. But January 29, 2006 she had been moved in a little over 30 days to #1. Our words have power. I had to be stripped of my mind, heart, speech, hearing, knowledge and wisdom in order to realize that I can speak things into existence.

Well we were very excited that Bray'Anna received her new kidney. The first 90 days were crucial. We were watching to see if any rejection occurred. Bray'Anna was doing well. We became closer and our relationship with God as a family became closer as well. Bray'Anna started back in the sixth grade. Things went well. She could not attend school for two months. The school she attended sent two teachers to my house four times a week to tutor her and keep her caught up till she was able to go back to school. I was forever grateful. 1 ½ years after the transplant, Bray'Anna began getting sick, we went to see her doctor and they immediately hospitalized her and did a biopsy on the transplanted kidney. Well the biopsy showed she was rejecting the kidney. I again began to fret because I thought all of this was over. My faith that I thought I was strengthening flew out of the window. All the Word that I was studying and preaching and teaching, a bit stronger, I may add, had left me so I thought.

Again I reverted back to my old ways. Worrying, depression and negativity had come back to be a part of my life. Why is it that all of this keep coming up and I could not exercise the power that I had on the inside of me?

One Sunday, I was really seeking God and I needed to hear a Word from God. Have you ever been in a place where it felt like God had stopped his hand from moving over you or throwing supernatural blessings over you? Have you ever been to a place where it felt like God had stop speaking to you? Well, I was at that place. I felt as though God had forsaken me. I was praying and nothing was happening. I was studying the Word of God and nothing was happening. I was not understanding what I was doing to stop the hand of God and shut the voice of God up. Well this particular Sunday, my previous Pastor, Overseer Billy Gore preached a message entitled "How Do You Receive the

Word?" He gave a demonstration of a glass and he poured a little water into the glass. He had someone bump into him and the water spilled out. This parable represented a person coming to Church but not in Church. The Word went forth, they heard it but were not doers of the Word and as soon as Church was over, someone cut them off going home and they began cursing them out and sticking their middle finger up at them. He started the process over but this time he added more water than before. This time when the person knocked into him, the water spilled out but a little stayed in. He gave the parable of you coming to Church and getting the Word. You are concentrating on the Word. You take notes and all but you are still allowing the enemy control over your mind. You are still worrying about the situation you are in, instead of allowing God to work it out. Worry has consumed you. The third time he started the process he filled the glass up till the brim and water was overflowing the glass. Even when he was bumped, water spilled but the glass was still filled up. The meaning of this one is you are studying the Word, hearing the Word, digesting the Word and Living the Word, when someone crosses you wrong, you will know how to handle it.

Immediately that message hit my spirit. Tears began to flow and I began to hear God speak to me during the message. God told me to hold my head up because He has deposited so much Word, Wisdom, Knowledge and Understanding on the inside of me. He also told me to concentrate on Him more because He cares for me. The moment I heard God say that to me was the moment Overseer Gore was making the Altar appeal. I got up out of my seat and went to the Altar for prayer and true repentance. I knew this was going to be a long road for me and yet I would go through it alone, but I also knew God had equipped me for this journey. There was nothing I was going to encounter that Jesus had not already gone to the cross for. I was finally at peace. When I realized that, I knew I had received all the wisdom and knowledge needed for this situation. On to more wisdom for other situations.

> **"My people are destroyed because they have not learned. You were not willing to learn. So I am not willing to have you be My religious leader. Since you have forgotten the Law of your God. I will forget your children."**
> **(Hosea 4:6 New Living Version)**

That is where I was. I had to repent because I was teaching others but not applying any of the law to my very own life. I was a hypocrite. When you are honest to yourself, that is when you can become free. That is when God can really strip you. I thank God for stripping me of my very own knowledge and wisdom and placing his knowledge and wisdom on the inside of me. We are so busy quoting Scriptures but not living the Scriptures. Remember the Book of James tell us to be Doers of the Word and not just

Hearers only.

"But be ye doers of the word, and not hearers only, deceiving your own selves."
(James 1:22 King James Version)

Seed Time And Harvest

"Who hath divided a water course for the overflowing of waters, or a way for the lightning of thunder; To cause it to rain on the earth, where no man is; on the wilderness, wherein there is no man; to satisfy the desolate and waste ground; and to cause the bud of the tender herb to spring forth?"
(Job 38:25-27 King James Version)

After Elihu finished speaking, God came forth out of a whirlwind to speak. He asked Job why are you confusing the issue? He told Job to get his self together and stand up and quit speaking on what you don't know. (That's a message right there for all of us. We speak about and on things we don't know. We add our two cents to people's situation without consulting God on their behalf. All we need to do is Pray and God will definitely handle his part. We call ourselves encouraging them but we do more harm than good.)

God told Job, He was going to ask some questions and He wanted straight answers from Him. He asked Job since, he has all the answers, where was he when He created the world and who decided on what size it would be? He asked Job how was the foundation poured and who set the cornerstones?. He told Job He did all of that. He was in charge of creation. He asked Job did he order morning and night, the oceans, light, darkness, snow, hail, lightning, the wind, rain or water to the deserts. God kept questioning Job. He asked do he know how the animals function? After God finished He asked Job directly, "What do you have to say?" He asked Job was he going to take him to court and press charges? Job apologized to God, he told God he was ready to shut his mouth and listen. (Many times we open our mouths and talk and we should not have said a word.)

God was still speaking to Job through the whirlwind. He asked Job to tell Him what he was doing wrong. He asked Job was he calling him a sinner and he a saint. He asked Job does he have the same power He does? Job immediately answered God by telling God He has all the power. He admitted to God he was wrong. All his life he was going on rumors he has heard about him but now he has firsthand experience. He really knows who God is. This time he really and sincerely understood God and he repented for real and worshipped God in Spirit and in Truth.

Have you ever had a true experience with God? Those true experiences should have caused you to really grow closer to Him. Job did not really appreciate God till He had a true encounter with Him.

My true encounter with God, you will probably say is doing those ups and downs concerning my daughter's health. Well NO! My true encounter with God came in the form of finances. Yes finances!

I have always been a giver. If I had it, you had it. If the Pastor or anyone if I be honest, asked me to sow a seed, I did. Not because I wanted to be big time or have my name called out but because they asked. And if I had it, they got it. When they asked and I didn't have it I got really upset and would get depressed for not having money. So depressed till I was literally sick because I could not give. People always use the Scripture God knows your heart. Many times I think people use it as a cliché instead of a

Scripture.

" Then he said to them. 'You like to appear righteous in public, but God knows your hearts. What this world honors is detestable in sight of God."
(Luke 16:15 New Living Translation)

"Do not look on his appearance or on the height of his stature because I have rejected him, For the Lord sees not as man sees: man looks on the outward appearance, but the Lord looks on the heart."
(I Samuel 16:7 English Standard Version)

"God who knows the heart, showed that He accepted them by giving the Holy Spirit to them, just as He did to us."
(Acts 15:8 New Living Translation)

"for the Lord searches all hearts and understands every plan and thought."
(I Chronicles 28:9 English Standard Version)

"For the Word of God is living and active. Sharper than any double-edged sword, it penetrates even to dividing soul and spirit, joints and marrow it judges the thoughts

and attributes of the heart."
(Hebrews 4:12 English Standard Version)

I studied these Scriptures and can quote these Scriptures and I thought I was doing things all right and I was going all wrong. My giving was not the problem because I had a heart of giving. Yes God knew my heart because I am a giver, a helper and will give my last, but where I was depositing was hurting me and not helping me.

I don't know how God speaks to you. God speaks to me through visions, dreams, sermons, people and through my very own prayers. One morning I was praying and seeking God, I told God I need more money to give and sow. During my prayer, God spoke and said everything will be alright. So I was content. Not long after this statement from God, I received an unexpected check in the mail for three hundred dollars. The check came from a previous client that owed me but never paid for their services. It came at a much needed time. I had bills that came in and did not have enough money to pay all of them, plus it was time for Bray'Anna's medication to be refilled.

That evening I went to a service and it was offering time. I knew that I really did not have anything to sow, but the person in charge kept asking for sowers to come sow. I began to think of my needs and decided I needed to sow, because I needed some things from God. Without thinking or seeking God I had sowed over ½ of what was allotted for bills and medication. I didn't worry because I knew God would take care of me, He always does. My faith was strong. After all I've been through with my daughter, my faith had gotten stronger.

I kept trusting God, well the time came and I still only had enough money for the bill or the medication. So of course the bill had to wait because my daughter's medication came before anything. I began getting a little depressed because if I was a sower, I expected to get money back. I did not quite understand then what I know now. I began throwing a pity party and always saying "Why does things always happen to me?" I began getting in a funk again. Why the continuous cycle? I was not walking in the fullness of God.

I was exposed to the Bible and the teachings but was my life changed by it? One day I was reading the Word of God and God took me to the Parable of the Sower in Matthew 13 chapter. While reading the chapter I heard God say to me before you can sow anything You must plow up the soil. In verses 3-9, a farmer planted seeds. While he was planting seeds some fell in the road and the birds ate them. Some of the seeds fell in the gravel. The seeds that fell in the gravel, did sprout but the roots did not sprout, so when the sun came out, the sprout withered away. Some of the seeds fell in the weeds. As those seeds sprouted, it was strangled by the weeds. Some of the seeds fell on good soil and a harvest was received. The meaning of the story was explained in Matthew 13:18-23. The seed that fell in the road and the birds gathered it up is compared to the Kingdom. You may be getting the Word but because you don't take the Word in, the enemy can come and pluck everything away, so that you don't get it and don't understand it. The seed that landed in the gravel is compared to the person that hears the Word and gets very enthusiastic about it while it is going on but don't really take it in. When the emotion wears off and the enemy attacks, he wins because you don't have the real word. You only have the emotions behind it. The seed that was cast in the weeds is the person that hears the Word but the materialistic things of life strangle you. You always want more and always worrying about having things. The seed that was cast on good ground is the person that hears, and takes the Word and apply it to their life. They will reap a great harvest.

My life was just like the seed that was growing in the weeds. I was planting but not planting in good ground. Everything I was planting was being choked by thorns and the sun was burning my seeds and they were withering away. I learned sowing was a good thing. I thought as long as I sowed, everything is good and I will reap a harvest. That statement is only 50% correct. It depends on how you sow and who you sow into. You may be sowing into someone, God has cursed. You cannot bless what God has already cursed, just like you can't curse what God has blessed.

"How can I curse, whom God hath not cursed? Or how shat I defy, whom the Lord hath not defied?"
(Numbers 23:8 King James Version)

I had to learn that even though sowing is a good thing, you must be careful where you sow. I was so confused at first because the Bible tells us

"But this I say, He which soweth sparingly shall reap also sparingly; and he which soweth bountifully shall reap also bountifully."
(2 Corinthians 9:6 King James Version)

"Be not deceived; God is not mocked; for whatsoever a man soweth; that shall he also reap."
(Galatians 6:7 King James Version)

There were so many Scriptures on sowing but I was taking the meaning of the Scriptures on but not as the meaning it was intended as.

I have lost many things because I was sowing time, talent, and treasures into people, places and things that God was not blessing. Money came but the hole that was in my pockets seem to lose it as I received it. There was nothing I could do with the losses either because God was stripping me of my sowing till I learned how to sow into fertile ground. In order for me to sow into fertile ground I had to learn to take God's word to heart and live the abundant life in the

Kingdom God has designed for me.

In the midst of my sowing I had to learn to place assignments on my seeds. Many times I was facing mountains of needs; spiritual problems, sickness, family problems, fear, financial issues, and a list of other things. I had many issues that I could sow for. I had to place my seeds against a particular need. How did I do that? First I had to identify what was the purpose of my seed sowing. Was my sowing because the man and woman of God in front of me was making a plea for a seed or was God trying to meet my current need because of my seed? Secondly I had to ask God about what I was believing in. Did I believe because of the Word of God or was I using God as a bank just to get what I want from Him then I needed to sow something? Thirdly my sow was a Seed of Faith.

"He said to them, 'Because of your little faith. For truly I say to you, if you have faith like a grain of mustard seed, you will say to this mountain, Move from here to there and it will move and nothing will be impossible for you."

(Matthew 17:20 English Standard Version)

Fourthly, I had to learn to aim my faith by using the Word of God against my situation. Lastly I had to learn to look to God as my source and not to men.

> **"I assure you that you can say to this mountain, May God lift you up and throw you into the sea, and your command will be obeyed. All that's required is that you really believe and do not doubt in your heart. Listen to me! You can pray for anything, and if you believe, you will have it."**
> **(Mark 11:23 New Living Translation)**

If you place your seed on a specific need and trust and believe God for that need, He will make it happen. Timing is very important though. I am an instant person. If I pay for something, I wanted my item immediately but that is not how God works. Have you ever prayed and prayed and nothing ever happened? When what you pray for doesn't happen, you begin to become weary. The Bible tells us

"And let us not be weary in well doing for in due season we shall reap if we faint not."
(Galatians 6:9 King James Version)

Continue to trust God in that situation. After you have sown that seed, cultivate it, work it, water it, prune it, nurture it and prune it some more, till it sprouts up. Bishop William Murphy III has a song that says "This is my season for grace and favor. This is my season to reap what I have sown. I haven't been perfect, but I have been faithful. God's got a purpose yes and I know he's able. I've got a seed in the ground, that He's blessing, no more stressing. I've got a seed in the ground, now I know Him I can show Him." The song says "I've got a seed in the ground." Your seeds will come up if you trust and believe. You cannot waver with your faith. God would not have had to strip me in this area if I did not waiver in my faith. This time this lesson has been learned. I trust God!

I'm In Love With A Stripper… Stripping At It's Best

I Need A Blood Transfusion

"Her young ones also suck up blood: and where the slain are, there is she."
(Job 39:30 King James Version)

I know, I know! What does a blood transfusion have to do with being stripped. It has a lot to do with it. A blood transfusion is a "medical treatment that replaces blood lost through injury, surgery, or disease. The blood goes through a tube from a bag to an intravenous (IV) catheter and into your vein." (www.webmd.com/a-to-z-guides/blood transfusion) Why are blood transfusions important? When you lose too much blood because of an injury or surgery, a blood transfusion is needed. If your bone marrow doesn't make enough blood such as "a plastic anemia" (web.com) you may need a transfusion. Just like anything else, too many blood transfusions can cause problems with your immune system.

There are different types of blood types; A, B, AB, and O. Each of the blood types can be negative or positive. If by chance you get a blood transfusion and it's the wrong type, you will have a transfusion reaction. That could be very dangerous and you must seek treatment immediately.

Blood is essential to life. No one can live without blood. According to statistics by the Mayo Clinic, about 25% of Americans will need a blood transfusion at least once in their lifetime. However, only 5% of individuals donate blood. If you have ever donated a pint of blood you have helped to save a life.

Jesus is just like that. Jesus had a conversation with his disciples. He told them unless you eat the flesh of Him and drink His blood, you have no part of Him. When you need a transplant and don't receive one, it could be very detrimental to your living.

In 1628, Sir William Harvey, who was an English Scientist, discovered that the blood was a "river of life" flowing around in the body. Doctors tried to replace lost blood with blood of other humans, and animals. Many times this had happened but the patients died. Because of the unsuccessfulness of this during the 17th century; laws were passed forbidding blood transfusions to take place.

In 1900, Dr. Karl Lansteiner, A German Scientist unlocked the mysteries to successful blood transfusions. He discovered that depending on your blood types, determines who you can donate too.

Blood speaks of life.

"A creature's life is in the blood. I have provided you the blood to make reconciliation for your lives on the altar, because the blood reconciles by means of the life." (Leviticus 17:11 Common English Bible Version)

What is the driving force of all physical life? It is blood! What is the source of everlasting life? It is the blood of Jesus Christ!

Blood also speaks of cleaning.

"If we claim that we experience a shared life with him and continue to stumble around in the dark, we're obviously lying through our teeth- we're not living what we claim. But if we walk in the light, God himself being the light, we also experience a shared life with one another, as the sacrificed blood of Jesus, God's Son, purges all our sin."

(I John 1:6-7 The Message Bible)

The purpose of human blood is to dispose waste, dispose of toxins and supply oxygen to your body organs. The blood of Christ also cleanses you from all sin and empowers you to have victory over the enemy and over sin. We are bought with the blood of Jesus.

The Blood of Jesus has the power to transform. When the blood of Jesus is applied to our lives, it transforms body, soul and spirit into a new creature formed in the image of God's holiness.

"Therefore if any man be in Christ, he is a new creature; old things are passed away; behold, all things are become new."
(2 Corinthians 5:17 King James Version)

When you are transplanted with the blood of Jesus, you are a new creature. Blood is our source of life. Without blood flowing through our veins life will end. We cannot survive without blood. Without the blood of Jesus applied to our spirit and soul we are bound and lifeless.

The blood of Jesus has the power to heal and protect. Whenever a virus attacks our physical body and begins to make us sick. Our blood begins to fight because the virus is attacking our white blood cells. When your body suffers an injury, a cut, our blood protects us from an infection because it begins to form a scab. The wound may be tender for a while and may leave a scar but you are protected so infection don't enter in through it. When the enemy of our soul rises up against us, the blood of our Lord and Savior covers us like a shield and destroys the enemy to protect our soul. Many times in our lives we suffer from different kinds of attacks on our Spirit, then the blood of Jesus wraps itself around our Spirit and our Soul to protect and heal all of the heartache we have experienced.

The Blood has the power to deliver. The blood of Jesus breaks the yoke of bondage of sin that attacks our body.

"Standfast therefore in the liberty wherewith Christ hath made us free, and be not entangled again with the yoke of bondage."
(Galatians 5:1 King James Version)

Whatever Satan has wrapped around your mind, body and soul, the blood of Jesus can set you free.

The first recorded blood transfusion involved Pope Innocent VIII. Three ten year old boys were promised a gold coin if they would allow a doctor to take some of their blood from them and give it to the Pope. It was not successful. The blood the Dr. took from the boys was injected into the Pope through his mouth. All participants, the Pope and the boys, died.

Afterwards, a successful way to inject blood intraveinously was created and now it is a successful form of treatment for those in need of blood. The American Red Cross has many blood service regions across the United

States. Many of us may never need a blood transfusion physically but Spiritually we all need Jesus' blood transfused into us.

> "But Christ being come an high priest of good things to come, by a greater and more perfect tabernacle, not made by hands, that is to say, not of this building; Neither by the blood of goats and calves, but by his own blood he entered in once into the Holy place, having obtained internal redemption for us. For if the blood of bulls and of goats, and the ashes of an heifer sprinkling the unclean, sanctifieth to the purifying of the flesh; How much more shall the blood of Christ, who through the eternal Spirit offered himself without spot to God, purge your conscience from dead works to serve the living God?"
> (Hebrews 9:11-14 King James Version)

We are cleansed through the blood of Jesus. Without having the blood of Jesus running through our veins, we have no part of being in the family of Jesus. We don't have to go to a Blood Bank to receive blood because there was a Blood Bank opened by

Jesus on the cross over two thousand years ago for us. We don't have to wait in line for it. Chemicals have to be added to our blood in our blood banks at the Red Cross to preserve it. There is no preservatives needed to be added to Jesus' blood. This blood is incorruptible and sinless.

"For as much as ye know that ye were not redeemed with Corruptible things, as silver and gold, from your vain conversation received by tradition from your fathers; but with the precious blood of Christ, as of a lamb without blemish and without spot."
(I Peter 1:18-19 King James Version)

Being stripped by Jesus and transfused with the Blood of Jesus is the best thing to ever happen to me. Every time I am cut or injured I say to God, "Thank you for the Blood of Jesus!"

Backlash

"And it was so that after the Lord had spoken these words unto Job, the Lord said to Eliphaz the Temanite, My wrath is kindled against thee, and against thy two friends: for ye hath not spoken of me the thing that is right, as my servant Job hath."
Job 42:7

After God finish speaking to Job, Job responded. Job stated how upset he was. He told God, he should have never spoken. He told God he was ready to close his mouth and just listen to Him. God immediately began to speak to Job again through a whirlwind. He asked Job was he calling him a sinner and calling himself a Saint? God told Job to show off his power. He told Job to stop the wicked and evil ones from doing what they are doing. After God finished this time. Job began to worship God. Job told God He was more powerful than anything or anyone. He apologized for just talking. After God finished with Job, he turned to Eliphaz, the Temanite and told him he was tired of him and his friends. He told him that he had not been honest with Him or honest about Him. He told him to take 7 bulls and 7 rams and go to Job to sacrifice a burnt offering on his behalf. Eliphaz, Bildad, and Zophar did what God commanded. God accepted Job's prayer. After Job interceded for his friends God restored all of his fortune and doubled it, his children he lost and his entire being.

I remember hearing a story of a lady that was about to get married. She was so nervous that she told her Pastor that she did not think she would be able to make it down the aisle. He told her to concentrate on the middle. And when she get to the middle of the aisle concentrate on the altar and when she get to the altar concentrate on her man. So while she was walking down the aisle she was repeating where everyone could hear her. Aisle, Altar, Him, Aisle Altar Him. She was saying what the Pastor told her to do, but all the audience heard was I'll alter him. Many times we are saying things right and doing things right but others perspective is totally different from yours and they are out to prove you wrong. Stay the course! Job's friends were trying to prove Job wrong which caused Job to doubt himself.

So many times when we enter into relationships we try to change the other party. It could be a platonic relationship or a relationship that we want to end up in marriage. We try to change people but that's not our job. That is God's job. Relationships are meant to be reciprocal. Relationship is defined in dictionary.com as "the state of being connected or related; association by blood or marriage; kinship; the mutual dealings, connections, or feelings that exist between two parties, countries, people, etc." We have formed many relationships and sometimes the relationships we have entered into keep us away from God. We hold people up as a god instead of the real and only God. And as soon as we hold them up as a god, they do something contrary and end up falling then we are hurt and don't know what to do next.

Backlash is defined by dictionary.com as "a sudden or violent reaction, forceful backward movement, recoil, bommerang; resistance; response." I had to be stripped of relationships. I had to be stripped from good and bad relationships. I did not hold people up as a God, but I allowed people that I was in relationships with, to use and abuse me so God had to strip some people out of my life. I have been in and out of relationships with the opposite sex but they could not stay because I was not allowing God to run the relationship. I have been hurt over and over again in relationships because I did not give God an opportunity to run them. God was not in control of my relationships.

Many of my relationships ended in a backlash because God will show you he is in control. Because of the treatments I received I learned to be in relationships and cover my heart, mind and soul so I would not get hurt. I did not learn to my latter years, meaning now, that I had to cover my body too. I did not realize everyone I had been in sexual relationships with became a soul tie to me. Your soul tie should be with God.

People are afraid of being hurt by other people, so they build up walls of protection around themselves. I am not speaking of what someone told me. I would do the same thing. The closer you get to people, the deeper these people can hurt you. We build up walls because we are afraid of being betrayed, laughed at, mocked, judged or abandoned. Because of this we avoid real community with other people. We may go to church, but we make sure to make a quick escape after the service, talking to no one along the way. People are held back from authentic community by fear. And that fear is being afraid of getting hurt.

"Do two people walk hand in hand if they aren't going to the same place?"
(Amos 3:3 The Message Bible)

"Can two walk together, except they be agreed?"
(Amos 3:3 King James Version)

We have to be very careful with the relationships that we enter into. As Christians we are recognized by a very distinguished mark of faith and that is the privilege we have to walk with Christ. We cannot walk with God if we are not on one accord with Him. God does not operate in disorganization. We must realize that the way we relate to other people have a strong bearing on our walk with God.

"If anyone says, I love God, yet hates his brother, he is a liar For anyone who does not love his brother, whom he has seen, cannot love God, whom he has not seen. And he has given us this command; whoever loves God must also love His brother."
(I John 4:20-21 New King James Version)

That is telling us in order for us to walk in unity with God we must first agree to walk in unity with one another. As long as there is division and strife among us as people, our fellowship with God is divided. To walk with God requires us to be within the boundaries of His will. His will dictates the necessity of His followers being united as one. Because of the things the division and the strife between some of the relationships I was involved in I was beginning to hate people. Yes I said HATE! Don't judge me! I know hate is a strong word but I am just being transparent. Hate is defined by dictionary.com as "to dislike intensely or passionately; feel extreme aversion for or extreme hostility; detest." It is the desire of God's heart for his people to be united. Unfortunately, satan has done a tremendous amount of damage by using people to cause division, strife and conflict. He has used those closest to us and they do not even realize they are being used.

For the longest time, I kept telling myself marriage is not for me. I tried it once. It didn't work and I was convinced it will never happen again. When we separate or divorce, we find every reason we can to blame the other on why it didn't work. Yes there are many reasons I can say it did not work on his behalf, but this book is about my stripping. First I married and knew we were unequally yoked. That was the number one mistake right there.

"Be ye not unequally yoked together with unbelievers

for what fellowship hath righteousness with unrighteousness? And what communion hath light with darkness?"
(2 Corinthians 6:14 King James Version)

My next mistake was not keeping things in divine order. My thought pattern was messed up. I knew God was head of my life but because I am a worker, server and lover of God, my top priorities were God, Church and family. I had it out of order. It should have been God, Marriage, Family and Ministry. In my marriage, I was putting everything even though he was out of order with God, before him. Two wrongs don't make it right. Your treatment of others cannot be predicated on how they treat you. Love is love!

Because my marriage failed I began to tell myself, I will find the right man this time! Mistake number 3. I felt as though I was looking in all the wrong places for a man because it was my desire to be married. No matter what Church I was going into, I was looking for a man. In the grocery store, I was looking for a man. At my children's football, basketball, softball or baseball games I was looking for a man. Because I could not find one I figured that fate would have it that I did not need a man in my life.

One day during my meditation, praise, and worship time, God took me to the Scripture.

> **"Whosoever findeth a wife findeth a good thing and obtaineth favour of the Lord."**
> **Proverbs 18:22**

God was telling me I was doing it all wrong. I was looking and the man is the one that should be looking for me. God stripped me of my mindset in order to be stripped of relationships.

God's love is unconditional and it is not based upon how we measure up. The same must be said about our love towards one another. Stop entering relationships based on conditions. If you do this for me, then I will do that for you. It does not matter if you ever do anything for me, if God commissions me to do something for you, count it done! I have to be obedient.

"Obedience is better than sacrifice."
(I Samuel 15:22 King James Version)

When we don't know how to love ourselves, we begin to look for love in all the wrong places which results in people that we think mean us some good, stripped out of our lives. I dated many boys/men because I was looking for love in them instead of loving the main source which is Jesus. During the stripping process of relationships, God took me back to the Scriptures.

"Nevertheless I have somewhat against thee, because thou has left thy first love."
(Revelations 2:4 King James Version)

I am not ashamed to say while I was married there were many times that I put my ex-husband before God. I would allow him to take the place of my time with God. I would allow him to make decisions on things God had already assigned to me. He was making decisions on things God had assigned to my hands. I stopped studying the Word of God and I am a professional student of the Word of God. On some occasions I stopped going to Church. Every awakening moment I was spending energy on trying to please a person that God never told me to marry. When you enter into relationships that God did not ordain, trust me He will let you know. You will begin to lose things, and feel like your life is falling apart. I am so grateful that I have learned to even put relationships whether sexually or platonic into the hands of God and allow Him to lead those relationships. Because of my disobedience to God many relationships I was in with people, generally had to close because I was having backlash from them.

God stripping me from relationships was the best thing to happen to me. He closed doors that I could not close and open doors and pushed me into doors I was too stubborn to walk through.

Binding and Loosing

"Thou shalt also decree a thing, and it shall be established unto thee; and the light shall shine upon thy ways."
(Job 22:28 King James Version)

"Wherefore seeing we also are compassed about with so great a cloud of witnesses, let us lay aside every weight, and the sin which doth so easily beset us, and let us run with patience the race that is set before us."
Hebrews 12:1 (King James Version)

This Scripture is telling us to set aside every weight that is holding us back. Weights are heavy and if you are not careful you will have a setback trying to hold on to all of those things that are not like God. We must learn to put away, and cast off every, and all burdens, hindrances and offences that can so easily beset us. Beset means standing around. If we are standing in a race and not running, we should never expect to win. You have to be in motion in order to be in the running to win the race. I don't care how many times you say, "I will win the race!" If you are not in motion you will not win the race.

Some of the weights that needed to be removed from my life and probably need to be removed from your life too are the weight of sin, the weight of the blame game, the weight of greed, the weight of jealousy, the weight of bitterness and the weight of laziness. These weights and many more keep us bound and stop us from being in the will of God.

"Verily I say unto you, whatsoever ye shall bind on earth shall be bound in heaven; and whatsoever ye shall lose on earth shall be loosed in heaven. Again I say unto you, that if two of you shall agree on earth as touching anything that they shall agree on earth as touching anything that they shall ask, it shall be done for them of my Father which is in heaven. For where two or three are gathered together in my name, there am I in the midst of them"
(Matthew 16:19 King James Version)

"And I will give unto thee the keys of the kingdom of heaven; and whatsoever thou shalt bind on earth shall be bound in heaven; and whatsoever thou shalt loose on earth shall be loosed in heaven."
(Matthew 16:19 King James Version)

We must really learn the principles behind binding and loosing. We have so much power and we do not even know it. Let me rephrase that. I have so much power and it took me a long time to realize that. I could never see myself the way God saw me. He see me as victorious but I saw myself as the victim. He see me as a winner but I saw myself as a loser.

It really took some stripping from God in order for me to let go of the strongholds that had me bound. Stronghold is defined by free dictionary.com as "an area dominated or occupied by a special group or distinguished by a special quality." Many of the strongholds that were holding me captive were jealousy, fear, low self-esteem, financial bondage, pride, my own body, bad habits, slothfulness, self-centeredness, unbelief, guilt, emotions, feelings, among others.

My sowing and planting had to be stripped because it was a stronghold. I told you in previous chapters that we have to be very careful and sow into fertile ground. You must take everything to God and He will direct you if you are discerning who and what to sow into.

> **"And that's not all You will have complete and free access to God's Kingdom, keys to open any and every door; no more barriers between heaven, and earth, and earth and heaven. A yes on earth is yes in heaven. A no on earth is a no in heaven."**
> **(Matthew 16:19 The Message Bible)**

We have been given all authority to bind and loose. We have the power to bind every stronghold that is holding us back. All we have to do is exercise the power that God has given us. If we are delivered from the many different spirits but leave the strongholds in place, they are liable to return.

The book of Ephesians tell us to put on the whole armor of God. However it must be stated that the adversary is always looking for a weak part in the armor. If you leave one piece off he will push his way in and set up a strong hold in your life. In dissecting II Samuel 5th chapter you learn believers are not meant to be overwhelmed by strongholds. Admit that you have strongholds present in your life. Too many people have made excuses to let their sins continue. Some say I will work on it tomorrow. Maybe next week or a month from now I will give it up. If you are going to win this battle, you must start today.

As a believer you have the authority to open (loose) the door of salvation and close (bind) it. As a believer you have the authority to lose people from sin and bind the habits that are holding them back. As a believer you have the authority to lose people from sickness and bind up the demons of sickness. As a believer you have the authority to bind false teachings and loose sound doctrine. As a believer you have the authority to bind the habits that help you and loose the ones that hinder you. Living a victorious and stripped life mean we have learned to exercise the authority to bind some things and loose some things.

To exercise your authority by binding and loosing, it is important to remember these Scriptures.

"Behold I give unto you power (authority) to tread on serpents and scorpions and over all the power (ability) of the enemy; and nothing shall by any means hurt you." (Luke 10:19 King James Version)

"Submit yourselves therefore to God, Resist the devil and he will flee from you." (James 4:7 King James Version)

"Be sober, be vigilant because your adversary the devil, as a roaring lion, walketh about, seeking whom he may devour. Whom resist streadfast in the faith, knowing that the same afflictions are accomplished your brethren that are in the world." (I Peter 5:8-9 King James Version)

When you resist the devil you have no parts of Him. You have on the full armor of God. Give him no place to work in your life.

Stripped

"So the Lord blessed the latter end of Job more than his beginning; for he had fourteen thousand sheep, and six thousand camels, and a thousand yoke of oxen, and a thousand she asses. He had also seven sons and three daughters."
(Job 42:12-13 King James Version)

"Then Job arose, and rent his mantle, and shaved his head, and fell down upon the ground, and worshipped, and naked came I out of my mother's womb, and naked shall I return hither; the Lord gave, and the Lord taketh away; blessed be the name of the Lord
(Job 1:20-21 King James Version)

To strip is defined by Dictionary.com as "to move, make naked, undress, to deprive or dispossess; to rob; to make bare, to take apart; to damage or to break."

It was not until Job repented and turned back to God, in spite of what family and friends were saying to him and about him. God restored Job with a double portion of everything.

When you allow God to strip you, and strip you totally, restoration is in store for you. It does not matter what's been lost. God will give you greater. Can God trust you with greater? He was able to trust Job with greater. Job received more than he lost. Get focused and stay focused so you can receive the greater of life. In His time, He will move in power in your life. Stop allowing everything under the sun to have your attention, except God. Someone reading has been looking and seeking the Lord for a breakthrough in your life. You have tried to find comfort in every one you have sought advice from. After you go through the stripping process, God will open the windows of Heaven and pour you out a blessing you will not have room to receive.

"But they that wait upon the Lord shall renew their strength, they shall mount up with wings as eagles; they shall run, and not be weary; and they shall walk and not faint."
(Isaiah 40:31 King James Version)

Job had it all. At least that is how it looked in the natural eyes until tragedy hit him and everything that was precious to Job was stripped from him. He was very successful until he became sick. His home was in shambles, his marriage was falling apart and his children were dead. One time or another we all will be stripped.

"Therefore we do not lose heart. Even though our outward man is perishing, yet the inward man is being renewed day by day. For our light affliction, which is but for a moment, is working for us a far more exceeding and eternal weight of glory, while we do not look at the

things which are not seen. For the things which are seen are temporary, but the things which are not seen are eternal. If you have Christ you are eternal."
(2 Corinthians 4:16-18 King James Version)

God will strip each of us of the temporal but not the eternal. I was missing out on the best things of life because I was striving for what was temporal.

Job learned to forgive his friends and repent unto God.

"Repent ye therefore and be converted, that your sins may be blotted out, when the times of refreshing shall come from the presence of the Lord."
(Acts 3:19 King James Version)

Job found hope in the future of God. After that God restored everything. He received double for his trouble.

I thank God for the process of being stripped. When God stripped me, He expected me to drop all that dead weight. I had to get rid of everything that had been slowing me down. I had some blessings that were held up. I had to get rid of everything and everybody that had been slowing me down. I was carrying folks that didn't want to be carried. Because they didn't want to be carried, I was carrying things that had me stagnated. If folks you are trying to help don't want to change leave them alone, they will hold some stuff up for you.

I am truly grateful for the stripping because I did not have control over the thoughts that would pop into my mind. Before the stripping, negative thinking. After the stripping positive thinking and casting down those imaginary thoughts as they entered my mind. We must remove all those things which confuses our progress towards Christ. We are to love one another with a pure heart. The things that we allow God to strip from us are the things that soil up our heart and dirty up our lives.

As believers we should be craving God's Word. Our yearning and craving more should be consistent. Your praying must be consistent. Your praise must be consistent. Your worship must be consistent. Your Intercessory must be consistent. Your warring in the Spirit must be consistent. Your studying the Word of God must be consistent. Your fellowship must be consistent. You must die to the flesh daily.

"For if you are living according to the flesh, you must die; but if by the Spirit you are putting to death the deeds of the body, you will live"
(Romans 8:13 New American Standard Version)

He strips us so we may be able to live pure and clean lives. He strips us so we may be able to conquer the temptations of life. He strips us so that we may be able to receive the promises He has made us. He strips us so that we can freely worship, praise and honor Him as we walk in this corruptible world. God just takes His word and feeds us, nourishes and nurtures us in His marvelous grace. As we crave and yearn for His Word

He grows us more and more into His image. You never know who may see that special light coming from you and want that same light. When we kill the flesh each and every day then that light comes forth and we can help bring another to that life that comes flowing from you. If we are to live daily for God it will require us to ask God to strip us daily. God has never abandoned us, so why do we abandon Him? When we are stripped we are free to demonstrate God's power and God's presence in us! Stripping is a necessity! There is a whole lot of stripping going on and I hope you are in line for the stripping because Stripping Is At It's Best, and please know I will always be in love with MY STRIPPER!!!!!

www.ingramcontent.com/pod-product-compliance
Lightning Source LLC
Chambersburg PA
CBHW022113040426
42450CB00006B/686